Appalachian Trail in Bits and Pieces

by

Mary Sands

9 781889 386256

APPALACHIAN TRAIL CONFERENCE
799 WASHINGTON STREET • HARPERS FERRY, WV 25425

ISBN 1-889386-25-1
Printed in the United States of America

Fourth Printing

For information or to order books, please write:
Appalachian Trail Conference
799 Washington Street
Harpers Ferry, WV 25425
(304) 535-6331

Dedication

I dedicate this book to "Papa," my number one fan
and husband, Paul Sands. His support and assistance
were positive influences.

Preface

This is an adventure story, not a how-to book. If you are interested in hiking with a group, consult the latest outdoor safety and environmental rules books. They are available at book and outdoor equipment stores. Also write the A.T. Conference at P.O. Box 807, Harpers Ferry, West Virginia, 25425-0807 for information about the Trail.

Acknowledgments

First, I want to thank the Kentuckiana Girl Scout Council for offering training in working with groups and safety in the out-of-doors, which gave me confidence to try. I also want to thank the volunteer trainers who stressed the importance of keeping records. Without those records I would not have had the material to write this book.

Many thanks to the volunteers who work to keep the Appalachian Trail a National Scenic Trail.

I am grateful to Joy Pennington, a professor at Jefferson Community College, who taught me, at age sixty, to write. She went over and beyond the call of duty correcting spelling and grammar, and she wore out many pencils, influencing me to make an active story.

Carolyn Fenn, a Girl Scout friend with a home computer, spent many hours typing manuscripts and using a heavy pencil.

Dotti Schultheis, another Girl Scout leader, contributed the line drawings.

Thanks to Karen Baechle Miller, a hiker and recipient of the Gold Award, which is the highest award a Girl Scout can earn, for her painting that appears on the front cover and the sketch of her hiking up the mountain on the rocks.

Thanks also to everyone who made suggestions and encouraged me by saying, "You can do it, one day at a time."

CHAPTER ONE

Early one evening my phone rang. The voice on the line said, "Are you Mama Boots?"

"Yes," I replied, "How did you know?"

"I didn't know your real name, so I called the Girl Scout Council and asked for the number of the lady called Mama Boots—the one who hikes on the Appalachian Trail with Girl Scouts."

"You have the right person," I told her. "My real name is Mary Sands. Can I help you?"

"I'm Jane Tharp, a Girl Scout leader. My troop wants to go backpacking and I need your advice."

"We're starting plans for a trip in April," I replied, "and we're having a meeting at my house on Thursday night. Why don't you come and bring your girls? They can learn about backpacking and decide if they would like to go."

"Great!" said Jane. "I'll start calling them tonight. I know they'll be thrilled."

As I hung up the phone, I felt a new surge of excitement at the thought of introducing backpacking to yet another group of girls. For eight years I'd been a volunteer consultant for the Kentuckiana Girl Scout Council, which includes a large part of Kentucky and several counties in Indiana.

I'd been a hiker since growing up in Pendleton County, Kentucky during World War II, when tires and gasoline were rationed and my parents could seldom afford to drive me places. As a teenager, on a Sunday afternoon, I

1

would walk five miles round trip to my girl friend's home. Following a creek down the hill, I trekked a game trail until I came to the road to her house. I stayed only a short time, then I'd start home. On these cool evenings I was in no hurry. I strolled along, savoring the silent, deep shadows of the woods and arrived home at dark.

I attended the University of Kentucky, where I met my future husband, Paul. After he graduated, we settled in Louisville and started raising a family. I never realized how much I enjoyed hiking until I stopped walking everyday, but family camping trips gave me a chance to relive my childhood walks.

In August, daughters, Diane, eight years old, Martha, thirteen, Martha's friend Patty, who was in Martha's Girl Scout troop, our son John, eleven, Paul, whom I fondly refer to as "Papa," and I left for a two week vacation to the Shenandoah National Park in Virginia. At the entrance gate, I asked the park ranger for a map of hiking trails. The ranger showed us where we could get on the Trail and hike about thirteen miles.

After setting up camp, Martha and Patty helped plan a day hike on the "A.T." or "The Trail," as it is called. I found a drawstring bag to carry our peanut butter and jelly sandwiches and a jar to use as a canteen. Early in the morning, Papa drove us to our starting point at Riprap Gap.

The Trail was well marked with six-inch rectangular blazes of white paint—on trees, rocks, or whatever was available. At first it was easy, mostly descending, but after lunch we started climbing. Not knowing what ascending a mountain was like, we climbed and climbed, thinking there was no end to the mountain.

Martha called, "Are you on top of the mountain yet? I'm getting thirsty and hungry. How much farther do we have to go?"

"I'm not on top," I gasped, "and I've no idea how soon we'll be there."

According to the map, the altitude was over 2,000 feet. The more we climbed, the hotter we got, and our drinking water was all gone. It was the hardest hiking we had ever tried. At the summit we found a big rock and sat down to rest in the breeze. Questions raced through my mind. Is this just a trail through the park or is it more? Where does it begin and end? Where can I find the answers?

Martha broke into my thoughts, and we continued toward camp, crossing over a bald mountain with the sun in the far west. Martha asked, "Are we there yet?"

I replied, "No, but the Trail is going down, so it shouldn't be long."

When we reached Rockfish Gap at the southern entrance to the park, I felt we'd hiked on an extraordinary trail and was eager to learn more about it. My muscles were sore, my feet ached and my body was stiff from lack of physical preparation, but my first hike on the Trail was the most satisfying hiking experience I'd ever had.

Immediately after returning home, I found the address of the Appalachian Trail Conference and wrote for more details. I was overwhelmed by the information. What a trail! Two thousand miles up mountains and along ridges, through valleys of farmland, across rivers, and on country roads following the Appalachian Mountain Range from Springer Mountain in Georgia to Mt. Katahdin in Maine, cleared and maintained by volunteers from hiking clubs near the Trail.

Joining the Appalachian Trail Conference, the organization which coordinates the volunteer activities of all the Trail clubs, I started receiving the *Trailway News*, a bi-monthly publication about the Trail and stories about hikers. I also received materials on backpacking equipment and supplies and information on how to plan trips.

In August, two years later, we planned a family vacation to the Smoky Mountains. I had a map of the Smoky Mountains with all the trails marked and noticed a trail which led up the mountain from Cades Cove and joined the A.T. at Spence Field on the ridge. I had borrowed some large day packs from the Girl Scout Council where I was a leader of Troop 116, Diane's Brownie troop, and put our bulky sleeping bags in the packs. There was very little space left for our food and cooking equipment.

Determined to try an overnight backpacking trip, Martha, Patty, John (now a Boy Scout), and I put the small overstuffed packs on our backs and left Cades Cove Campground, following the trail leading to the A.T.. We had planned to hike to Clingmans Dome, twenty-one miles away, and spend the night halfway at Derrick Knob Shelter.

We were used to hiking, but not with heavy packs and never at altitudes between 4,500 and 5,000 feet. Breathing became very hard. Our backs hurt; our knees felt like rubber, and something seemed to pull us backward. After five miles, I decided we needed better equipment and more physical conditioning before we could successfully backpack. We returned to camp disappointed, but still determined to hike on the A.T..

The next day Papa and I, with some camping neighbors, hiked up to Thunderhead Mountain and back. Papa wasn't an enthusiastic hiker, but he agreed to go with me. This time I set a steady pace and gradually managed to get to the top without being completely exhausted. Thunderhead Mountain was the highest mountain I'd ever been on—5,530 feet. I looked at the adjoining mountains and Cades Cove. What satisfaction to know I'd gotten here using my own physical power.

I still wasn't satisfied about not hiking a full day on the A.T., but getting up to the Trail was a problem. Then I remembered a riding stable in the park. Patty, Martha and I found that we could rent horses and ride to Russell Field. Wranglers would return the horses to Cades Cove.

While hiking, we met a backpacker, whom I bombarded with questions about backpacking and the A.T., and he offered to let me try on his pack. The pack weighed much more than our little packs we had carried on our aborted trip, but because of the well distributed weight and the snug fit, it was easier to carry. As Patty, Martha and I continued on to Fontana Dam, where Papa would pick us up, I kept thinking about how much I wanted to try backpacking.

I liked working with Diane and the Brownies, but backpacking was for older Girl Scouts. A backpacking program could help girls learn more about themselves and the world around them, develop personal skills, and learn to be self-sufficient. They could set goals and strive to reach them. I knew I had to get involved in the Girl Scout program beyond my troop. Excitement surged through me, and I was even more determined to learn all that I could.

I sent for every free catalog available, read every book I could find about backpacking, outdoor safety and survival, and ordered the guidebook to the Smoky Mountains from the Appalachian Trail Conference.

The following year I still needed to build confidence, so Papa, John, Diane, and I went to Cosby Campground in the Smoky Mountains in July. On a magnificent day hike to Davenport Gap, I kept talking about my plans to go backpacking and tried to encourage them to go with me. When Papa discovered that I had borrowed a pack for him, he went along with my plans. Diane was eager to go, but she was too young to carry a pack, so Papa and I carried most of the equipment in the two big packs, and John carried a small pack.

On the second day of our vacation, we made arrangements with a camping neighbor to drive our car back from Newfound Gap where we would start hiking. We packed some freeze-dried trail food, supplies and clothing in preparation for an early start.

We put on our ponchos and started up the mountain in the rain. By lunch time we'd reached Charlies Bunion, a large rocky outcropping. The rain had stopped, but it was still cloudy. I'd forgotten to make our sandwiches for lunch, so we had peanut butter and jelly on the breakfast doughnuts. Backpacking was going to teach me how to improvise. We couldn't see the view because of the clouds, but John threw a rock, and we listened for it to hit the ground far below.

We went on to Pecks Corner, hiking farther than anticipated on this first day. Pecks Corner is one of a chain of three-sided shelters or lean-tos, spaced about a day's hiking distance on the Trail, with wooden floors or wire bunks for sleeping six to ten hikers. The shelters usually have spring water, a fireplace, picnic tables, and latrines. Fences stretch from side to side and from ground to ceiling in front of the lean-tos in the Smokies to keep out the bears. I felt more comfortable about backpacking, knowing the shelters would provide a safe place to sleep. A couple of bears came to visit, adding much excitement to our evening. We felt very brave behind the wire fence when we retired for the night.

As clouds blew around the trees and down the mountain, we walked through the middle of them, and Diane shifted our attention to the trees and forest floor covered with green moss. As we finished lunch at Tri-Corner Knob Lean-to, another bear strolled up and looked around, then walked away. We continued on to Mt. Gyot, where the wind chilled us.

Later, we arrived at Cosby Knob Shelter, thinking we might spend the night, but a group of Girl Scouts from Charlotte, North Carolina, occupied the shelter. We rested for awhile, and I asked the counselor questions about how to plan hikes on the A.T.. The group was a camp unit. My hiking group would have to be found in a different way because I didn't have the whole summer free to be a camp counselor.

Papa broke into the questioning by reminding me that we needed to get back to camp before dark. Early that evening, we arrived at our campground. I had read all the books and had wondered what it would be like to spend a night out on the A.T., carrying what we could on our backs. I had wondered about the weather, the bears, and our physical endurance. But now I had confidence that the girls could meet the challenge of the Trail and that I could meet the challenge of safely leading the girls on the Trail.

CHAPTER TWO

I called the Girl Scout Council three years after my first introduction to the A.T. and talked to the program specialist. She was delighted with my decision to be a volunteer backpacking consultant and started describing my duties, which would include allowing the girls to plan and carry out responsibilities.

"At this time the Girl Scout program doesn't include backpacking," she told me. "You and the girls will have to set up your own guidelines and submit them for approval."

"How can I let the girls know that I'm available to help them?" I asked.

"Send a notice to the Senior Girls through the Senior Planning Board," she said. "I think the girls will be quick to take advantage of your offer."

Fifteen attended the first meeting, and I shared with them the experiences I'd had on the A.T.. "Would you like to plan a trip?" I asked.

Margaret replied, "I only came because my mother thought backpacking would be a new adventure, but now that I'm here and know more about it, I'm ready to go!"

Several girls expressed their interest. They elected officers and got down to the business of what they would need to do in order to make it happen. "Where can we go to hike?" asked one of the girls.

"Wherever you want," I assured her. "We don't have to hike on the historical Appalachian Trail. We can find a shorter, easier one to start on if you wish."

"But I want to hike on the A.T.," Ellen said. "I've hiked on a lot of shorter trails; the A.T. would be more exciting."

"My parents are planning a trip to the Smoky Mountains the third week of August," Sandy said. "They'll help with transportation if we hike in the Smokies then."

Sandy's mother, sitting in the back of the room, concurred. After much discussion about when everyone would be available to hike, the group agreed that August was a good time and that they would like to be able to say they'd hiked on the A.T. in the Smoky Mountains. The girls then decided to hike south from Newfound Gap to Spence Field, twenty-three and a half miles.

As the girls looked over a personal equipment list of the bare necessities, they discovered they already had some items, such as mess kits (cup, spoon, plate), ponchos and flashlights, and I asked them for suggestions on how they thought they might remove some of the weight from their packs.

"Every ounce counts when you are carrying everything on your back," I advised, "so if you can do without it, leave it."

"Plastic jars are lighter than metal canteens, and we can take one large tube of toothpaste and one large bar of soap for the whole group," Peggy P. suggested.

Margaret asked, "Will one change of clothes be enough?"

"Yes," I replied, "but bring extra socks, so you can change if they get wet, and bring a sweatshirt or windbreaker for cool nights." Sandy asked, "Will we need new sleeping bags?"

"Good question! If you have a lightweight one, that will be fine, but put it in a plastic bag or 'stuff bag' in case of rain. Keeping your sleeping bag dry is very important."

I advised everyone to take some first aid training and talked about primitive camping skills. It became apparent that the girls were well-trained in this area. Explaining that we would be setting up our own guidelines, I gave them some of my equipment catalogs and asked them to read some backpacking books that were on the A.T. Conference book list. We decided to meet again in two weeks.

The girls opened the meeting with a vote to take freeze-dried foods and decided to use #10 cans for cooking. They discussed what they had learned about boots and the care of the feet. The Council had bought new backpacks with padded shoulder straps and hip belts for the program, and I advised them on how to pack in order to balance the weight. For backpacking, I told them, a good rule to follow is to carry only 20 percent of your body weight. Before adjourning the meeting, we made plans to take a conditioning hike.

7

During our hike of 12-8/10 miles in Clark County Forest, Indiana, we discussed first aid equipment. Everyone would carry a personal first aid kit, including insect repellent and a bandanna. This lowly item would come in handy as pot holder, washcloth, or even a bandage.

As we hiked, I reminded the girls that a Girl Scout always leaves a place cleaner than she found it. I shared with them a motto I had heard from the Sierra Club: "When in the wilderness, take nothing but pictures and memories; leave nothing but footprints, and kill nothing but time."

This triggered a question from Peggy, "Will there be snakes on the Trail?"

"You may not see them," I said, "but they'll probably be there. The best protection against a snakebite is to leave them alone and watch where you put your feet and hands. If anyone should get bitten, we will immediately get off the Trail and find medical help."

The preparatory hike gave us confidence, and the big day arrived. On August 17, ten girls, fourteen to seventeen years old, left with Papa and me for Cades Cove, Tennessee. Papa had surprised me by asking if he could go along. I hadn't expected him to like backpacking so much. On this trip, the girls started calling Papa and me "Papa and Mama Boots" because I insisted that everyone wear hiking boots.

The group of girls were very compatible. Vi, a high school senior and the oldest girl in the group, had good leadership skills. Peggy was a high school track star. Margaret, with a beautiful voice and a large repertoire of songs, was our song leader. Patty, who had been along on our family's hike in the Shenandoah Park, was the only girl with A.T. hiking experience. Bonnie C. was a zealous Girl Scout, and Bonnie H. had a nice easygoing, even personality. Ellen, who exuded a quiet confidence, and Joris, who had worked as a day camp aide, were close friends. Sandy was very sociable and articulate, and the exuberant Kim was the youngest of the group.

The girls decided it would be interesting to keep a log of the trip, so they could share the experience with friends. Their account of the first day:

> Arriving at Cades Cove by two P.M. Saturday, our group set up camp, removed the packaging from the freeze-dried food and finished packing our packs. We put the packs on and took a short hike to check fit, weight and balance before retiring for the night. A bear visited our camp during the night and rooted in the empty boxes looking for food. At one time during the

ordeal, Mama Boots imagined that the hairy creature was actually inside the tent with her.

It was a long night because I was afraid the bear would find the packs with our food. I hadn't realized that freeze-dried food would have enough odor to attract bears.

The sun was shining, and the day was perfect for hiking. Our first day would be only 6-1/2 miles and the girls sang and chatted as they walked along a well-graded, but steep, trail.

At high altitude the forest floor was green with wood sorrel, which the girls had never seen before. The trees and moss-covered rocks prompted Kim to describe the forest as "a green fairy land." She said, "I expect a little green fairy to fly by any minute." Kim was only fourteen years old with a delightful personality and was determined to see every thing new and different in our wilderness environment.

On arriving at Mt. Collins Shelter we hung our packs from the rafters to protect them from bears and gathered wood for our supper fire. We had started eating our first meal, ham and au gratin potatoes, when some boys came in and informed us that all thirty-two of them planned to spend the night. The shelter, with two wire shelves, or bunks, was made to accommodate twelve people. Six people could sleep comfortably on each bunk. How would it be possible for all these people to sleep in the shelter?

The boys, who were younger than the girls, spent the evening throwing firecrackers, making catty remarks, and generally aggravating the girls. I don't know whether this was the boys way of communicating with the girls, or whether they thought that if they annoyed us enough, we would leave, and they would have the shelter to themselves.

When night came, the twelve of us squeezed onto the top bunk. We didn't want to sleep outside because we thought bears might be around. The boys crowded onto the lower bunk and on the ground in front of the bunks. One boy had a hammock which he strung up above the boys on the ground. Every time anyone moved, the next closest person was disturbed, and a chain reaction occurred. Someone was moving all night long.

When I saw light, I slipped out to watch the sun rise. The pink sky through the tall pine trees in the quiet still of the early morning was refreshing. We had survived our first night on the Trail. I was so grateful I said, "Thank you."

I wasn't worried about the girls, even though they had butterflies in their stomachs, wondering about what to expect and what a full day of backpacking would be like. I had no doubt their determination and good camping skills would see them through any problems we might encounter.

Kim wrote in the log:

> We arose early to start hiking toward Clingmans Dome, the highest point on the Trail (6,643 feet). There we ate lunch and sang "Mr. America" to Papa Boots as he walked to the top of the observation platform. We happy wayfarers resumed our hike toward Silars Bald. About 1-1/2 miles before we reached Double Spring Gap Shelter, two boys caught up with us, adding color to the trip.

Jim and Dave were about the same age as the girls. When we arrived at Double Springs Gap, we found a few of the thirty-two boys who had stayed at Mt. Collins. They told us they were going to stay at Silars Bald, the next shelter. Not wanting to spend another night in such crowded conditions, we decided to stay at Double Spring Gap Shelter. Dave and Jim stayed also. We had plenty of time to fix our supper and do the Girl Scout "harr dance," a dance similar to a chorus line, in hiking boots. Stuffing a towel into a canteen cover for a football, the group played pass the ball. We ate wild blackberries and watched Fontana Lake in the distance. Other hikers joined our happy, fun-loving group. Margaret and Sandy, who had good voices and knew many songs, led the group in singing. The music must have put the bears to sleep because we never heard any around.

"Who has the soap?" asked Ellen. "Patty," replied Joris, "and she's already gone."

"Whoops!" I thought.

Shortly after we left, we came to a semi-overgrown knob with a view of the mountains that we would be climbing later. When we reached Silars Bald Shelter, Dave and Jim were there cleaning up the mess the thirty-two boys had left. As we continued on, we met some people going the other way on the A.T., and they told us the boys were already set up at Derrick Knob Shelter.

I called a meeting of the group and first reminded them that if they had the soap or the toothpaste, they shouldn't leave camp in the morning until everyone had a chance to use it. I also told them that according to the guidebook, the next five miles made up a rough, steep trail and required considerable exertion but that the large group of boys already occupied Derrick Knob Shelter. "What do you want to do?" I asked.

10

Ellen, one of the older girls in the group who had logged considerable mileage on day hikes, echoed the feelings of the group. "I'd rather hike five more miles than be so crowded in the shelter."

Early in the afternoon we marched through the group of boys like an army on its way to victory. The boys let out disappointed sighs, and I heard a few say, "They're not going to stay with us." The rocky, steep ground hurt our feet, and breathing was hard, but no one complained.

Kim, a good story teller, wondered aloud about what it would be like to live on top of the mountain. Her story made the struggle go faster and kept us from thinking about our sore feet and aching legs, and we reached the top of Thunderhead Mountain by four o'clock in the afternoon.

Thanks to some blackberries along the Trail, we managed to ward off starvation. I had discouraged the girls from bringing snacks because I thought the smell of food would attract bears. But after this trip, all of us would carry some gorp—which is a mixture of dried fruit, nuts and seeds, or other high energy foods.

Peggy, nicknamed "Pigtails" because of her braids, and I were the first at the Spence Field Shelter. I suggested she start fixing supper, and I returned to help the slower hikers. Sandy had sprained her ankle, and Bonnie H. felt sick in her stomach, but everyone made it. Peggy was a good cook, and we all revived with her hot beef stew.

Other people were at the shelter, but the girls were willing to sleep on the ground. I wanted to hug every one of the girls. My worries had been unnecessary, and my prayers had been answered. Since the girls were ahead of their plans, and they were doing so great, I wondered if they would want to go over Gregory Bald.

We got a good look at a bear in the early daylight. The people sharing the shelter had hung a pack between two trees, and the bear wanted it. Standing on its back paws, the bear kept swatting at the pack. Each time the pack didn't fall, the girls gasped and cheered. After about three tries, the pack fell and everyone scared the bear away.

After the excitement was over, I asked, "Girls, would you like to hike over to Gregory Bald? We have enough food and time." Jim and Dave thought that would be a good place for them to quit hiking also. With very little discussion the girls voted to spend the night at Mollie's Ridge Shelter and finish the Trail over Gregory Bald.

The group was busy packing sleeping bags, eating breakfast and getting ready to start hiking when the bear returned. I grabbed a plate and beat it with a spoon. Each girl followed suit, and we soon scared the bear away.

Everyone set a steady pace, and we got to Russell Field in plenty of time to relax while we ate lunch. It was our first opportunity to talk among ourselves without a lot of other people around. I asked the girls how they felt about the previous day's hike.

Sandy said, "Even with my sore ankle I'm glad we hiked on."

Ellen added, "I think it made a more interesting trip to do a long day. I feel I've really backpacked in the mountains."

"It wasn't all that bad," Peggy remarked, "but I wish we could have stayed longer to watch the sunset at the big rock on top of Thunderhead Mountain."

When we resumed hiking, a young boy passed us and the girls' hearts skipped a beat thinking he was one of the thirty-two. But the boy told Patty that he was with a group of seven. We all sighed because we knew the shelter would sleep both groups. Kim wrote about the evening:

> We were joined by a group of well-mannered boys who participated in the games we suggested, such as "this is a cat." We sat around in a big circle and passed a spoon which we call a cat. As we passed the spoon, we gave our name and repeated all the other names. That way, everyone learned every one else's name. Margaret, who loves to sing, asked Mama Boots, if we could put another piece of wood on the fire and ask the boys to sing along with us.

Jim and Dave, along with boys and girls who were strangers a few hours earlier, joined in songs around the campfire, closing with "Taps."

When all was quiet, my thoughts turned to the serendipity of the evening. Boys and girls had learned to communicate, sing and play games together. Singing around the campfire had given them a friendly bond. I hoped both groups would remember the experience as a very tranquil last evening on the Trail. My fears about taking girls on the A.T. were gone. I'd shared my love of being in the wilderness, and the girls had learned to cope with steep mountains and rocky trails.

Our last day on the Trail, while hiking on Gregory Bald, we saw a rattlesnake which Papa encouraged to move. As we continued down the mountain to the car, Joris and Ellen, who had been rather quiet on the trip,

13

started singing, yelling and laughing as they neared the car. "You're getting too much oxygen at this altitude," I laughed, "It's affecting you like laughing gas."

"Wahoo! What a great feeling!" Ellen laughed. "I survived! I reached the tops of the mountains, hiked a thirteen mile day, and I did it with only as much as I could carry on my back."

We were on an emotional high. The girls had learned about backpacking, coped with unanticipated problems, gained self-confidence, and exceeded their original hiking goal by fourteen miles. Our first backpack trip was so successful that I knew we would soon be planning another trek.

CHAPTER THREE

We took our first backpacking trip outside a national park in June. Kim and Bonnie H. were now experienced trekkers. Laura T., Nancy, Debbie F., Molly and Ann were on their first trip, and this would be the first time that Diane, now eleven years old, would be carrying a pack with her share of the food and equipment. Diane was smaller and younger than the other girls, but she'd heard so much about backpacking that her big blue eyes twinkled as she prepared to go on her first real backpack trip. We would hike forty-five miles north from Hampton, Tennessee, to Damascus, Virginia.

Late in the afternoon we reached Hampton and stopped at a service station to ask about a place to leave the car for a week. Mr. Carden, who lived close to the Trail, said we could leave the car in his driveway and offered to drive me to the Trail. We were meeting many helpful people along the Trail.

At Carden's Bluff Campground in Cherokee National Forest, Laura, Nancy and Debbie put up our family-size tent while Kim and Molly put up their tent. A drenching rain during the night soaked our tents. Not wanting them to mildew, we left them up while we hiked. It required two trips to get the eight girls and our gear to the Trail. I parked my car at Mr. Carden's house, and he drove me to the Trail.

The Trail outside a national park wasn't much different at first, but we soon discovered that the rainy spring season had promoted a healthy growth of weeds. In places they were as high as our heads, making us feel like trail-blazers. We approached the Laurel Fork Shelter, and Laura came running back shouting, "There's no latrine!"

15

At camp, they had used primitive latrines but never had to make their own. I showed them how to make a small hole in the ground, called a "cat's hole," behind a tree away from camp and told them to cover the hole after using it.

The shelter had a wooden floor, no bunks and very little space in front, and the spring was quite a distance from the shelter. The girls chatted happily as they gathered wood for our cooking fire. Nancy and Debbie found pink salamanders near the spring and had a great time watching them crawl over their hands and back into the leaves.

By nightfall the clouds rolled in, and during a hard rain, much to our surprise, the water ran down in front of the wooden floor, forcing us to grab our packs and put them up higher. The rain stopped and the girls quieted, but I kept hearing a noise in the woods. We were a long way from the Smokies, but I wondered if it could be a bear. The beam from my flashlight revealed nothing, and I finally convinced myself that it was my imagination. We were in complete wilderness, seeming to be the only people on the Trail.

The Trail was easy to follow but so rough that Debbie was getting blisters on her feet. "Daddy insisted I wear his army boots, but they're too big and too heavy," she said. "He said they would be better protection against snakes, but these hurt with every step. I'll never let him talk me into this again."

At Watauga Dam, the caretaker told us the Trail was steep and badly rutted at this point, the result of a forest fire, and advised us to stay on the road. Road walking was uncomfortable in hiking boots, but our relief at getting back to the Trail was short-lived. The path was overgrown with blackberries and nettles. The blackberry briars scratched our legs raw.

"Ouch! Mama Boots, my legs feel like they're on fire," cried Molly. "I can't stand this."

"It's the stinging nettles," I replied. "Let's see if I can find some jewelweed. The juice from the jewelweed will neutralize the acid from the nettles. Here's some; it's the plant with the little orange bloom. Rub the juice from the stalk on your legs to relieve the pain."

By the time our legs stopped burning, we found ourselves in weeds over our heads. "What happened to the Trail?" Nancy asked.

"I don't know," I answered. "Look around for a blaze."

"Could this be the Trail?" Laura inquired. "The weeds are broken down over here."

"Here's a blaze on this post!" Kim called. "It's a good thing someone else hiked through here or we'd be lost forever."

16

When we arrived at Vandeventer Shelter, Ann and Molly followed the blue-blazed trail that should have led to water but came back saying, "We can't find the spring."

"Well, it's supposed to be there. Let's check the guidebook," I suggested.

We read that we would have to follow two trails to find the spring. Gathering up all the empty canteens and cooking pans, Diane, Laura, and I followed the rocky, steep trails that the guidebook said led to water. We had to dip water out by the cupful from the small spring, and it took a long time to fill all our containers.

Getting back up this mountain with open pans of water was quite a trick. Diane, Laura, and I, each had a container of water plus full canteens. Balancing like tightrope walkers, we cautiously stepped around rocks and under limbs, watching every step, so we wouldn't slip and spill our precious cargo. I vowed we would have water containers with lids on our next trek. The 3/4 of a mile trip took us over an hour, and I reluctantly announced that the water was for cooking only, not for brushing teeth or cleaning up.

We were tired and discouraged. Our bodies had the lingering odor of sweat and a gritty feel of dirt that was coupled with the sickening smell of insect repellent on our stinging, scratched legs. Our backs ached from a day of bush-whacking through weeds and blackberry bushes, but the big rock behind the shelter provided a delightful place to recuperate. The finger-like Watauga Lake, which spanned the length of the valley, laid placid under the twinkling stars as we watched miniature car lights going up the road to a little town in the valley.

To avoid carrying another day's food supply, we intended to hike twelve miles. Mid-morning we came to an area where dead trees stood like giant skeletons, and big logs blocked the Trail. A forest fire had left its ugly scar. Climbing over the big logs felt like constantly mounting and dismounting horses. Without trees, the blackberries and nettles were thicker than ever. Kim voiced what we were all thinking. "Next time, I'm bringing long pants—no matter how hot it is."

We reached a gravel road and couldn't find the blazes indicating whether the Trail went right or left. We chose left. For half a mile we hiked without seeing a blaze. A car stopped and I asked the driver, "Is this the A.T.?"

"No," he said, "Hop in and I'll take you back up the mountain."

The remainder of the Trail to Double Spring Shelter was easy to follow, and we had learned not to go very far without seeing those familiar white blazes on the trees.

17

The next day we doctored our scratched legs as we chatted and laughed about getting lost. Kim and Molly were going to a party on the weekend after we returned to Louisville, and Kim asked, "Will these scratches heal by then, or will I have to wear stockings?"

"I really don't know, Kim," I replied. "Maybe they will if you don't get any more scratches."

Diane was proving herself a real trooper on her first trip. She had kept up or was ahead of the group and never complained. Her enthusiastic determination gave everyone inspiration.

At McQueen Knob Fire Tower we climbed up to view the mountains and guessed at the names. Nancy decided one should be called "Blackberry Mountain." A large body of water prompted Ann to ask, "Is that still Watauga Lake?"

We looked at the map and found that it was Holston Lake. Reluctantly we climbed down the fire tower and made our way to Abington Shelter. After supper we had a song session with a group of Boy Scouts who were also hiking the Trail.

Completely relaxed after our last evening on the A.T., I slept unusually well. The laughter of the girls woke me, and they kidded me about snoring. We walked into Damascus and headed to a store for some ice cream and Coke to make Coke floats. Mr. and Mrs. Dietrick, Ann's parents, had driven my car from Mr. Carden's to Damascus. When we got back to the campground, we found our tents still standing. Donning our bathing suits, we took a swim in Watauga Lake to celebrate the conclusion of our trek. Did that cool water ever feel good on our scratched legs.

On a repeat trip three years later, thanks to the hard work of the volunteers in the Tennessee Eastman Hiking Club, we found the spring had been enlarged, the Trail had been cleared of blackberries and nettles, and the big logs had been cut.

*   *   *   *   *

A year after our first trip from Hampton to Damascus, Papa, Diane, four high school girls and I drove to Erwin, Tennessee, and started hiking toward Hampton, sixty-two miles north. Lita was the only one who had not hiked with me on the A.T., but I'd backpacked with her and her troop in the Daniel Boone National Forest in Kentucky.

The McConnells, Kim's parents, took us from the Rock Creek Campground to the bridge that crosses the Nolichucky River. The Trail follows the bank of the Nolichucky, crosses under a railroad bridge, then turns and ascends Jones Branch. The water rushed over the rocks with breathtaking quickness. Little white bubbles formed as the water pitched from one rock to another. Over the little ones, around the big, it raced down the mountain. On its climb up the mountain, the Trail left the stream much too soon.

We reached the shelter too early in the day to stop. In the hot afternoon sun we followed the Trail on a gravel road just below a bald ridge. By four o'clock Diane and Lita came to a little meadow called Beauty Spot where we put up plastic to use as tents, a new addition to our equipment. On the way to the spring, Laura found a patch of wild strawberries which she and Diane picked to add to our instant vanilla pudding.

After a sound night's sleep, we started hiking on the gravel road again. We saw a blacksnake, a chipmunk, and a rabbit before leaving the road. As we rested on the summit of Unaka Mountain, I noticed Laura was crying. "What's the matter?" I asked.

She answered, "My stomach hurts, and I wish I could go home."

Laura was a quiet person, and this was her second backpack trip, so I felt she must really be sick. I gave her some Pepto-Bismol tablets, and we talked about what she had been doing earlier in the summer. When she began to feel better, we trekked on.

We reached Cherry Gap Shelter much too early to stop for the day. Kim got the guidebook to see if there was another place to stay. She read about a Mr. Montgomery, who allowed hikers to spend the night. The group decided to continue on and see if we could sleep in his yard.

Early in the afternoon we came to a tree filled with ripe sweet cherries. "Diane, if you got on Papa's shoulders, do you think you could reach those big ones on the branch right above your head?" Papa helped her up on his shoulders, and she handed down cherries to Kim, Papa, and me, then ate a handful herself.

Ann, who had found a limb she could reach, asked, "How come the cherry tree is here? Did someone plant it?"

"The tree was probably planted a long time ago when a home was here," I speculated.

After eating our fill of cherries, Kim and Ann, who were hiking in front, came to the road that led to Mr. Montgomery's house. As they approached, they noticed high weeds.

"Oh no," Ann wailed. "The house is vacant!"

Laura wondered, "Can we stay here anyway?"

"We'll have to find a spring for some water before we can stay," I answered.

Papa hunted around for the spring and called, "Here's some water. Do you think it'll be all right to use?"

"I sure hope so," I replied. "Lita has found a place to put up the plastic shelter."

I took the water jug and headed toward Papa through the tall weeds, and we filled the jug with fresh cool water from the spring.

I heard Kim's voice, muffled by the weeds, "Here's an outhouse. It's hard to get to, but at least it's a building."

Lita and Diane put up tents, and the rest of us fixed supper. By this time, Laura had improved and no longer wished to go home. Ann was walking around the house when she discovered a loose window and asked, "Mama Boots, can we sleep inside the house, out of the rain? I can get this window open."

"Crawl through and see if you can get the door open," I answered.

She crawled through the window and opened the door. Laura and I handed packs to her while Kim, Lita, and Diane finished the supper dishes. The old house was a dry place to spread our sleeping bags.

As we started to settle down for the night we heard strange noises under the floor and in the chimney. Not believing in haunted houses, I started hitting the floor, and the noise stopped. Then, the noise got louder in the chimney. My logic told me there must be mice, or rats under the house and a bird in the chimney. I had scared the mice, and when it got dark the bird settled down.

Kim read the guidebook, and tried to determine how far we would have to hike before we could stop for the night. None of the possibilities sounded promising. We couldn't find the spring that was supposed to be near the foundation of another old house. When we reached Hughes Gap there was no water and no place to camp. It was four o'clock, and in front of us was Roan Mountain, a climb of over 2,000 feet. It would take at least three hours to reach the next promise of water and a place to camp.

"Girls," I said, "we really don't have a choice. If we take it one step at a time, we'll get there."

It began to rain, and the Trail became muddy and slick. Our mettle was really being tested. After two hours of climbing what seemed like stairs leading into the sky, I caught up with Diane. It was almost six o'clock, and there was still no sign of an end to this long climb. Diane was very worried. "Mom, where are we going to sleep and fix supper now that it's raining? I'm awfully tired and hungry, and it's getting dark."

"One step at a time, Diane. We'll find a place," I assured her.

After another hour of struggle, we reached the summit of Roan Mountain, 6,285 feet. The rhododendron bushes were in full bloom, a breathtaking sight. As I started back down the Trail to meet the others, I heard a distant call. "Mama Boots! Where are you? We're lost!"

I shouted back, "Keep coming! I hear you but I can't see you."

We continued to call back and forth until we were together again. They were relieved to know that they were near the top of the mountain, and Laura started telling me about their struggle.

"We'd take three steps up, then slide back two in the mud. Ann had cramps and started crying. I think we all would have loved to just sit and cry, but we knew that if we stopped we could sit there 'til we rotted or the bears came and got us."

Kim chimed in, "We were sure glad to hear your voice."

By the time the girls finished the stories of their hard climb, we had reached the top. They gasped, and their faces looked stunned when they saw the rhododendron ablaze with blooms.

"I can't believe this," Laura exclaimed. "This is really awesome. Here I was, wondering how I could've been so stupid as to want to backpack on mountains, when BAM—my God! This is the most beautiful place I've ever seen! I'm sure glad I didn't go home."

Rhododendron bushes as large as garages, covered with pink, lavender, and purple blooms the size of softballs, were so close together they seemed to form one large bush that covered the entire mountain. The area was having a festival, and a couple of boys were there protecting the portable concession stands. They let us cook on their stove and gave us stale cotton candy and Pepsi. We spent the night in the rest rooms. An unusual place perhaps, but it was still raining, and the rest rooms were dry.

Ann quipped, "I like to be close to the bathroom at night, but having it right by my head is ridiculous."

Kim suggested, "Let's drive back to see this again after we finish our hike."

Amid clouds and rhododendron bushes we crossed the gap and hiked up Grassy Bald, looking back at every opportunity to see Roan Mountain, pink with blooming rhododendron. Grassy Bald had large bushes of orange azaleas and pink mountain laurel. While resting, we pointed to the distant mountain and bragged about being there the day before. We were ahead of our original hiking plans and had no idea where to find water or a place to camp. As we hiked, we could see Roan Mountain from every viewpoint. To make sure we weren't going in circles, Lita got out the map. The Trail went north, then west, which meant that Roan was the mountain we were seeing across the gap.

By four o'clock we still hadn't found potable water. We were in the gap below Hump Mountain, a bald mountain where cattle grazed. Kim and Laura sighed in unison, "Oh, my gosh, do we have to climb that mountain?"

I replied, "I hope not! Maybe the Trail goes around the side."

About that time Papa spied Diane's red pack on the mountain. We groaned. The trail going around the side was a cattle path. A cool breeze made the climb easier, and when we reached the summit, we had a magnificent view of Doe River Valley and more mountains in the distance. We couldn't find the spring mentioned in the guidebook, but it wasn't far to Pink Winter's home, a friend of A.T. hikers. By six o'clock we arrived at his house. He showed us the spring and told us we could camp in the nearby field or in his garage.

Ann asked, "Why don't we sleep in the garage?"

We were awakened early when Mr. Winter started backing his truck into the garage in order to turn it around. Lying on the floor, we thought he was going to back over us, but he drove off without hearing our screams.

We ate breakfast at King of the Mountain Truck Stop in North Carolina. Fresh eggs, pancakes with real syrup, fresh orange juice and milk, what a treat! It really perked us up for the rest of the trip. We restocked our food from the grocery before resuming our hike. The Trail followed a road to Sunset Orchard and then along a fence. Hiking was on numerous small ridges, and we crossed several fences before we reached Moreland Gap Lean-to for our last night on the Trail and our first night in a lean-to.

We began early and soon came to a beautiful falls, the largest I had seen on the A.T.. Located in Laurel Fork Gorge, the falls cascaded a hundred feet over layers of rocks and boulders resembling a large washboard. We rested here for an hour, cooling our feet in the water. From there the Trail followed the gorge on homemade bridges and skirted the base of a cliff on built-up rock walks at the edge of the stream. In places the Trail was actually cut into the side of the gorge. It was tricky hiking, but we had fun trying to keep our balance and not fall in the water.

Ending another trip, we'd learned that the Trail was more challenging, but less crowded, outside the national park. We'd found new ways to improvise shelter and to use the maps and guidebooks.

As we walked along, Kim reminded me about going back to Roan Mountain to see the rhododendron. There among the elegant bushes, I could hear the girls talking.

"There were times I didn't think I was going to make it," Ann said to Kim, "but now I don't want to go home. I like the feeling of knowing I can rely on myself and survive with what I've got in my pack. I've accomplished something on my own. I wonder if we can get Mama Boots to help us plan another trip next summer?"

"We can ask her," said Kim. "Where would you like to hike?"

"It doesn't matter as long as its on the A.T.," replied Ann.

CHAPTER FOUR

The adventures of the girls on the A.T. spread quickly through the Council and beyond. At the slightest hint of encouragement, their enthusiasm bubbled forth as they told of their endurance on the strenuous climbs, their courage when encountering bears and snakes, and the feeling of exhilaration on reaching the tops of the mountains.

M.S. (Mary Sue R.) a Girl Scout Leader and Cotton (Kay S.) a camp nurse, joined the girls and me in planning our June trek. We selected a forty-eight mile section from Allen's Gap, where North Carolina Route 208 merges into Tennessee Route 70, north to the Nolichucky River, near Erwin, Tennessee. The Schoolers, parents of Julia and Lita, helped with the transportation.

For safety, no one was to hike alone, and the leading hikers would stop at eleven o'clock to wait for everyone to catch up, so we could lunch together. As we started the steep climb of over 2,000 feet, some were hiking very slowly, others were snacking on blackberries, and several were bounding along like mountain goats.

All day Melody grumbled. "This is stupid! How could anyone possibly think that shoving one foot in front of the other with a heavy pack on your back is exciting?"

At Jerry's Cabin Lean-to, Corky (Carolyn H.) and Charlie strung up our tube tents which were like huge garbage bags with both ends open. With the help of Sheryl and Lisa they threaded a rope through each tent and tied it between two trees. Diane and Laura gathered wood. Jenny J. from Charleston, West Virginia, and Molly built the fire, and soon the spicy aroma of "Mama Boots Stew" filled the air.

This section of the Trail follows the North Carolina-Tennessee border and crosses several bald mountains with long steep ascends. M.S., Charlie and Bonnie C. sang, "Up we go into the Wild Green Forest, Up we go into the sky..." From the tops of the balds we could see for miles, one ridge of mountains after another. Some girls stopped long enough to admire the view, but their primary focus was making it up the long, steep climbs.

Jenny read in the guidebook, "ascend steeply," but didn't read the mileage. Spending most of the day climbing mountains, the girls decided the guidebook was completely wrong. It began to rain, and they wanted to set up camp without water, but I trusted the guidebook which read that a spring was a fourth of a mile down the mountain.

Melody complained, "Stupid, stupid, stupid! I can't believe how stupid this is! Anyone with an ounce of brains should be able to see how stupid this is! If I ever get home I'll never do anything like this again!"

Listening to Melody's tirades wasn't improving my disposition any, and I growled back, "You're beyond the point of no return. You chose to come on this trip—no one forced you. Quit your complaining and make the best of it. At least when you get home you'll be able to say you accomplished something, even if you don't like what your doing."

We found the spring and everyone pitched in to set up camp. It was late after our twelve-mile hike, and we needed to get set up before dark. Although we were in a completely isolated area, it was hard to find places for our tents. The rain had stopped and Corky, Ann U., M.S. and Charlie decided to sleep under the stars.

The diverse and occasionally conflicting personalities of the hikers tend to surface by the third day. I think of it as "personality day." The novelty of hiking has faded, muscles are sore and everyone is short on patience. This day was no exception. The fast hikers stopped at eleven, and it was one-thirty before everyone caught up. Everyone was hungry and angry. As we ate lunch in a meadow, we discussed the situation—that each person's pace was different, some wanted to look around more, while others wanted to cover ground quickly. I encouraged the speedy hikers to wait more patiently and the slower hikers to pick up their pace so that lunch could be earlier.

From the meadow, we could see the top of Bald Mountain and a big black cloud coming toward us. Trudging on in the rain, we headed for the top of Bald

25

Mountain where I came upon Melody sitting on a big rock in the middle of the clouds. To my surprise, she was smiling. As I sat down beside her, she asked in an apologetic voice, "Mama Boots, can I go with you on your next backpack trip?"

I had been ready to throw in the towel, but when you witness a girl overcoming negative feelings, gaining confidence in herself and opening her eyes to the beauty of the world around her—well, it's as good a feeling as being high on mountains.

In the ghostly clouds, unable to see anything but the ground under our feet, we blindly stumbled over rocks. Holding hands, we formed a human chain and Kim, the leader, searched for a blaze on the rocks in the grass while the last person in the chain stood on the blaze. Like a giant inchworm, Kim led the rest of us in a search for the next blaze. Suddenly Kim yelled, "I'm not going any farther. I'll walk out into space. I can't see anything but a white wall."

The groping seemed to go on for hours before we saw trees with the familiar blazes. Finding a spring and making camp for the night, Kim suggested "Alleluia" for our supper grace. We were very thankful we hadn't fallen off the mountain.

The rain blew into our tube tents and soaked our sleeping bags. With three in a tent, the condensation alone was enough to drown us. As we tried to settle down for the night, M.S. made us laugh when she said, "I feel like a human sponge. In fact, I feel like I have diaper rash."

The wood was soaked, and a backpack stove was not part of our equipment. Starting the day with very little breakfast, our emotions were as low as the clouds on Big Bald Mountain. We had blisters, rashes, stomach aches, and muscle pain and hadn't been dry for two days.

The rain stopped and Donna and Ann D. built a fire to dry our sleeping bags when we reached No-Business Lean-to. After dinner we had a "Scouts Own," a special Girl Scout ceremony created to express and celebrate the spirit of Girl Scouting. It was a time for reflecting and expressing feelings about nature, friendship, love, God and other mature subjects. Ann D. began by saying, "Tonight is our last night on the trail, and we're all still friends."

"It sure was rough the third day when everyone was mad, wet and silent," said Lita.

"Joining hands and making a chain to get through the clouds made us forget about being angry and taught us how dependent we are on each other," added M.S.

Ann smiled and said, "I'm sure glad none of us was hurt. We should all be thankful."

"It's a good feeling to forgive each other," Kim said. "We have to understand that we all have different personalities and reasons for being here, so we need to make allowances for those things."

Melody laughed. "I can't wait until the next hike, even though I was the biggest grouch there was on the first few days of this one. That feeling I had on top of Bald Mountain is hard to describe—it was worth all the troubles we had to go through."

We sang and tried to finish our song to the tune of the Air Force song:

> Up we go into the wild green forest,
> Up we go into the sky.
> Up we go along the rocky pathways,
> Up we go, do it or die.
> Up we go into the wild green forest,
> Trudging along, taking a risk,
> Going up and up and up and up
> and maybe someday we'll even come down."

We could hear the thunder rolling through the mountains coming closer and closer until it was right above us. Everyone lay in their tents and listened; we were already wet. At last the rain ceased, and we fell asleep to the music of the thunder echoing through the mountains.

A young man, Joe, started hiking with us and his presence perked up the spirits of the group. The sky cleared, and when we reached Cliff Ridge Overlook, we stopped to rest and watched the Nolichucky River wandering through the countryside with a train running along beside it. A hawk sailed through the air, and the little town of Erwin sat calmly on the banks of the river. We began to forget the earlier problems of the trip as we toasted in the sun.

The Schoolers picked us up, and we went to the Boy Scout office in Johnson City, Tennessee, to buy our A.T. hiking patches, then returned to the K.O.A. campground where we cooked a meal of fresh hamburgers and corn on the cob, and had ice cream for dessert.

As the girls prepared a campfire, I had to marvel at the power of the Trail. Emotions had come full circle. There was the excitement as we piled into the vehicles at the start of the trip, knowing little about one another. We felt anger at being kept waiting for lunch when we were starving and at having to walk longer than we wanted. The fear of falling off the mountain forced us to cling to one another and develop teamwork for the safety of all. Now, we had the pride of helping each other accomplish a common goal and the warmth of new friendships born in the realization that we could trust each other with our lives. We closed our campfire with a big friendship circle, crossing arms and holding hands with the person on either side, making a very tight circle. We sang "Green Trees" and "Taps," before retiring under the picnic pavilion where we knew we'd stay dry.

*　　*　　*　　*　　*

Kentuckiana Girl Scout Council wanted to offer a backpacking unit during resident camp in the summer. The camp director asked me to be a consultant and accompany the girls on the trip. Six girls registered for the unit. Melody and Bonnie C. were experienced A.T. hikers while Jeane H., Jody, Pam and Janet were on their first trek. M.S. and Charlie were counselors for the group.

The girls met with M.S. and Charlie at camp and made the necessary preparations for a forty mile hike on the A.T. from Mt. Collins Lean-to, south to Fontana Dam. Loading into the Council van, Papa drove us to the Smoky Mountains. We told Papa "good-bye" and hiked the short distance to the lean-to where we spent the first night of the trek.

The girls grudgingly crawled out of their warm sleeping bags to start hiking on a wet, slippery, winding trail that made its way through the clouds. As we approached the observation tower on Clingmans Dome, Jeane asked, "Can we run up the tower?"

M.S. replied, "Go for it!"

The clouds cleared in the afternoon and Jody bragged, "Look back—that must be Clingmans Dome. We've sure come a long way."

The girls wrote about our experience at Silars Bald Lean-to:

> We arrived at the lean-to at three-thirty in the afternoon to find it occupied by two fellows from South Carolina and one very skinny dog which we named Gulliver. That night Gulliver howled and howled, trying to warn us of a bear. The two played tag until Gulliver finally outsmarted the bear by sneaking up behind him and running him head-on into the wire fence that was stretched across the front of the lean-to. Nose

28

and pride equally damaged, the bear left, and we got to sleep
the rest of the night.

Charlie had read, the week before, about a boy sleeping under the stars
who was mauled by a bear at Derrick Knob. The remains of his sleeping bag
were still laying around. It was obvious by the expressions on the girls' faces
that they had a new awareness of the danger posed by bears. No one was
interested in sleeping under the stars.

The ambitious hikers left me far behind, which prompted me to call them
"mountain goats." Jeane and Jody lead the group up Thunderhead Mountain
with an increase in altitude of over 1000 feet on strenuous trail. The entire
group made it in record time without a puff—well, maybe they took a couple
deep breaths. Thunderhead was surrounded with clouds, but from Rocky Top
we had an extended view of mountains, ridges and Fontana Lake, which we
shared with Chuck and Warren, two school teachers.

After a long rest we continued on to Russell Field Lean-to. The girls
account of our evening:

> Chuck and Warren joined us in singing old and new songs and
> playing games like Ghosts, Stink Pink, Buzz, Thumper (which
> Warren taught us), Aunt Tilly Williams, and This Is a Cat,
> This Is a Dog. It was an evening which answers the questions
> "What am I doing this for?" and "Why am I racking my body
> like this?"

Moving along at a rapid pace, the girls in front stopped to study fresh
looking bear tracks on the path. They looked up to discover a big bear staring
them in the face. Jody and Jeane turned around with ghostly pale faces. "Oh my
gosh," Jeane gulped. "There's a bear. What do we do?"

"Get some plates and spoons out of your packs," M.S. suggested.

"It's probably the bear that hangs around Molly Ridge Lean-to looking
for food," I said. "The bear knows we are here but let's not startle him. If the
bear charges, beat on your plates as hard as possible. If he keeps coming,
throw your plates at him. I'll drop my pack, and while he searches for food
we can get away."

29

Silently we passed the bear like a toy percussion band ready to explode. Luckily, we didn't have to throw our plates and food away. Walking on to Birch Spring Gap Shelter in the bright sunshine, Jody suddenly stopped in mid-stride and said quietly, "Bonnie, there's a rattlesnake."

Sure enough, a big rattler lie curled at the edge of the path. Undisturbed, he continued his nap while we passed far on the other side.

At Birch Spring Shelter, we had a Scout's Own. We talked about why it was important to preserve nature and what it meant to be in good physical condition in order to take part in an activity such as backpacking.

Making a speedy exit down Shuckstack Mountain, we arrived at Fontana Dam before Papa. The girls suggested a tour of the dam. When we returned, Papa was waiting. Quickly changing into clean clothes, the girls were on their way back to camp, bragging about their exciting adventures.

Jeane commented, "The rest of the girls at camp will never believe the things that have happened on this trip—a steep mountain in record time, two bears and a rattlesnake."

*   *   *   *   *

Our plans complete, Surf (Terry M.), a camp counselor, Papa and I, our son John, and eleven girls squeezed ourselves and our gear into the Girl Scout Council van and a station wagon for our August trip. We had elected to hike from Davenport Gap, at the northeast end of the Smokies, north to Allen's Gap.

Our first full day of hiking started with a six mile climb up Snowbird Mountain. Joy gasped, "Mama Boots, I can't catch my breath!"

"Take it one step at a time and give your body time to adjust to the thin air," I advised. "Set a steady pace; don't try to rush."

"Is it time for lunch yet?" asked Lisa. "I'm hungry!"

"No," I answered, "but let's stop for a ten minute break. A drink of water and some gorp would taste very good. It's a hot day!"

Anna said, "Those girls who didn't come to the meetings aren't very friendly."

"I excused them from the meetings because they were at resident camp," I answered. "I hope they'll remember that it can be fun to make new friends and work as a group to accomplish a common goal."

As we continued our climb, my thoughts were with the group. The girls came from many different communities in our Council and didn't know each other well. I hoped their Girl Scout training and the magic of the Trail would

31

mold them into a team. The top of Snowbird Mountain, cleared of trees for satellite tracking equipment, provided an unrestricted view of the surrounding mountains. The beauty of the world made my concerns seem trivial.

Sitting around our campfire at Deep Gap Lean-to, I told the girls about an experience on a previous hike. "A fellow hiker started calling to the owls, 'To whoot—to who.' One owl answered, then another. The distant answers, 'To whoot—to who,' continued as we drifted off to sleep. In the early morning hours the owls came so close to the shelter we could hear their wings flapping as they flew through the trees above our heads. Since owls are birds of prey, I was relieved when daylight came."

"What's for breakfast?" yawned Jenny E. as the light of day woke us.

"Icky oatmeal and cocoa," responded Dean. "Were you expecting pancakes and scrambled eggs?"

"I don't know what's worse," said Anna. "The icky oatmeal or the grody freeze-dried beef! What's for lunch?"

"Spam on rye and M & M's," responded Kim, smacking her lips.

From dawn to dusk, food is always on the mind of the backpacker, either the delicious food you look forward to at the end of the hike or the "icky", "grody" trail food. Backpack food tastes better than it sounds and is the topic of much conversation. The longer you hike, the better it tastes.

"Oh! Look at all the Black-eyed Susans and sunflowers," said Lisa. "I've never seen so many in one place."

"Blackberries!" squealed Diane.

"Oh, oh!" shouted Kim. "Last one up the trail grab Diane, or we'll have to wait forever for supper!"

Late in the afternoon, we came to a picturesque stream with overhanging trees and decided to stop for supper before continuing on to Walnut Mountain Lean-to. While Kim, Joy and Melody fixed supper, Diane went up the mountain to a big patch of blackberries and brought back a plateful of berries to add to our oats for breakfast. Jeane H. and Jenny hiked ahead to the lean-to and came back with the news that the lean-to was already crowded.

"There's a level place behind the lean-to, and the weather is nice. Can we sleep there under the stars?" asked Jeane.

"Put it to a vote," I responded.

All agreed that they didn't want to put up the tube tents, and Kim remarked, "Those tents aren't any good."

During the night, I heard a loud grunting sound that seemed to come from the direction of the berry patch. "Oh my gosh, is that a bear?" I thought.

Listening for a long time and hearing no more sounds, I decided the bear had found enough berries in the patch and had gone on.

Snuggled down in our sleeping bags in the cool night air with the stars watching over us, we were unaware of the deep fog engulfing us. Without the morning sun to disturb us, we slept later than usual. Some of the girls refused to get up to help with the breakfast chores and a heated discussion broke out. Anna remarked, "You wouldn't get up and while Mama Boots was doing your job, you not only ate your breakfast, but you ate hers too."

"Well," one girl responded, "we were hungry!"

Melody replied, "Well, Mama Boots is hungry too and backpack trips are supposed to be a group activity."

I asked the girls to remember that everyone was tired. We all needed to reach down for the energy to do our part and not leave the responsibilities to someone else. The group's atmosphere was very cool as we left the campsite. Kim tried to distract us by pointing out the leaf skeletons and mushrooms of all colors along the Trail.

We arrived at our destination, Deer Park Lean-to by mid-afternoon and a family was there. They shared the lean-to, so we could take a nap after our strenuous hike, and the girls who hadn't done their chores in the morning offered to be the sanitation engineers of the evening. It was a good beginning toward healing the rift, until they decided the plates would make great frisbees.

The steep descent to Hot Springs, North Carolina, was hard on our knees, but the ice cream and candy from the little grocery gave us energy for the eight mile climb up Rich Mountain. At a small spring, some rested while others climbed a nearby fire tower where we could see Mt. Mitchell, the tallest mountain east of the Mississippi River.

On the last 2-1/2 miles to Spring Mountain Lean-to, the wildflowers were higher than our heads. Kim and Melody found spring water, down a unique triangular-shaped gap covered with ferns. A group of Boy Scouts, who camped up the hill, joined us for songs after supper.

"The last day of icky oatmeal," shouted Lisa as we arose.

"I'm so hungry," said Melody, "the oatmeal tastes great."

Anna and I were hiking together when she asked, "Why did those girls come backpacking? They never acted like they wanted to be part of the group."

"I don't know. There are all types of personalities," I answered. "Maybe they were just tired. They apparently weren't expecting to have to accept responsibilities on this trip. Backpacking on the A.T. requires a determination these girls don't seem to have. I hope that after this trip, they will be more cautious in deciding what they want to do."

"Well, I've had a good time, and it feels great to reach our goal," Anna added.

Reaching the parking lot at Allen's Gap, there were cheers, hugs and congratulations. "Can we take a hike during spring break in April?" Jeane asked. "There wouldn't be any bugs, and it wouldn't be as hot."

CHAPTER FIVE

Troop 116, my troop, was now a Senior troop and planned a four day hike for spring vacation in April. The weather could be unstable, anything from very hot to very cold, and there was always the possibility of rain. Barbara, a Girl Scout leader and Lisa's mother, also wanted to hike and offered to help with the transportation. Shuttling the car was always a problem. I hadn't been able to train my car to come to me when we finished hiking. People along the trail would help, but sometimes they were hard to contact. With two cars, we could park one at the Mt. Collins parking lot and the other at the end of the trek, an ideal situation.

Laurie, who had been on two other hikes, was our secretary for the trip. She wrote:

> What you are about to read is true; no names have been changed to protect the innocent because we are all guilty of backpacking in the first degree. We, all fourteen of us, drove to the Sugarland Visitors' Center in the Great Smoky Mountains National Park. On arrival, we found our group was too large. The Park Service has a policy of issuing camping permits to only as many people as the shelter will hold on any given night. The group had to be split or not hike in the Smokies. We decided to split the group.

Getting our permits from the ranger, we drove up the mountain toward Clingmans Dome. At the parking lot, a half mile from the Mt. Collins shelter, we found ourselves in a brisk, icy wind and thick, wet clouds. Barbara and six of the girls, taking their share of the food and equipment, were to hike north from Mt. Collins Shelter. The other six girls and I drove to Davenport Gap to hike south. We stopped at Laurel Spring Motel for Mr. Valentine, so he could bring the car back to his house and park it. Hiking a mile in the cold wind, we were surprised to find two people at Davenport Gap Shelter—Tom from Illinois and Ed from Virginia.

After breakfast we hiked out of the gap and up five miles. When Melody and Jeane H. got to Mt. Cammerer trail, they walked a half mile on to the fire tower, a building sitting on the point of the mountain. It wasn't what we normally thought of as a fire tower.

We came to Cosby Lean-to at about five o'clock. Our chefs for the evening, Debbie S., Anna, and Melody prepared spaghetti and meatballs, applesauce and lemonade. After supper we sat by the fire and talked about problems between girls and parents.

Jeane said, "I don't see why we have to be home at a certain time. I hate telling my friends I have to go home."

I tried to explain. "Parents want to protect their children from unknown mishaps. They don't want you hurt, and they have a hard time realizing that you're probably capable of taking care of yourselves. Remember, having teen-age children is a learning experience for them."

Debbie replied, "How can we learn about life if we're never beyond our own home? The only time I go anywhere is with family. I want to learn about what goes on other places."

"Well, you're not with family now," Sharon said. "It might not be as exciting as a party at a friend's house or a hamburger at Mac's, but it sure is different."

Melody added, "I'm glad my parents set limits. It shows they love me."

Anna commented, "It wouldn't be all that much fun if someone tried to hurt you on the way home late at night."

We woke at sunrise to a clear day. Our goal was False Gap, sixteen miles away. This was a long, hard day, and to top it off, Laurie got sick. I sympathized and pushed her up the steep mountains. Jeane was the first to complete the seven miles to Tri-Corner Knob Shelter, and I was close behind her. Jeane said, "How far back are the others? We need to hurry. We should meet Diane, Jamie and the others in Barbara's group pretty soon."

36

I replied, "I'm worried about the wind blowing Anna off the mountain. She weighs only ninety pounds. You wait here. I'm going back to see if everyone is okay."

About that time the girls appeared. Anna laughed, "The wind is blowing so hard the ground moves from the pressure on the trees. I thought sure I was going to be blown away when I crossed those bald spaces. I think my boots helped hold me down."

"Mama Boots," Sharon asked, "What is that on the trees? It doesn't seem to be snow, yet the trees are covered with an inch of white frozen stuff."

"The moisture in the clouds has frozen on the trees," I replied.

"It sure hurts when it hits you on the head," Anna commented.

The rain turned to sleet, and the wind, at gale force, blew it right into our faces. Knowing we would meet Barbara's group helped keep up our spirits, but by late afternoon we were getting concerned. Where could they be?

After what seemed like years of sleet stinging our faces, wind whipping our packs, and bits of frozen cloud bouncing off our heads, we reached False Gap Shelter. "Girls, get out of your wet clothes and into your sleeping bags to get warm. I don't want you to get hypothermia."

Anna asked, "What's that?"

"It's a condition where body heat is lost faster than it's produced," I explained.

"Do Jamie, Mary and the others know about hypo-whatever?" asked Anna.

"I hope so," I answered.

Sharon questioned, "Do you think we should go back and look for them?"

"No, it's dark, and we wouldn't be able to see them. We'd be putting ourselves into a dangerous situation and that wouldn't help them," I replied. "We'll just have to have faith that they're all right."

After a while, Sharon and I braved getting out of our warm sleeping bags to fix supper. A backpack stove had been added to our equipment. It took a long time to get it started but once lit, we soon had hot food. We put on all the dry clothes we had and prepared to sleep two to a sleeping bag. As we listened to the wind howl through the trees, we wondered about Barbara's group. Were they warm and safe? Had they had a warm supper?

We woke at five o'clock to something new—three inches of snow. The clothes we'd hung to dry on the front of the lean-to were frozen, and so were our boots. I lit the little stove and cooked some oats, then we used the stove to thaw out our boots. "Does Barbara's group have a stove?" asked Melody.

"No," I answered, "but they have Sterno, called 'fire in a can.'"

Anna's pants were frozen stiff, and she didn't have another pair. Jeane had shorts and some wide adhesive tape. Jeane put on the shorts and taped her legs—a ghastly sight—and gave her long pants to Anna. Everyone found something dry to wear, and we hiked out of the gap, up to the trail. The wind blew until the bent trees looked as if they'd break. Snow in our faces felt like knives. When we came to Charlie's Bunion, a large hill of rocks sticking out on the side of the mountain, the wind was even stronger. Jeane yelled, "Help! I'm going to blow away." Sharon grabbed her just in time.

We had to move fast. At Ice Water Spring Lean-to, three guys from Michigan gave us hot chocolate and showed us a quick way to light the stove. We decided to spend the night in the rest room at Newfound Gap and try to find Barbara's group the next morning. However, Jeane, in her shorts and taped legs, went out to the road where Nick and Emily Walkingstick, an Indian couple, and their dog Brownie, stopped. Jeane explained, "We're a group of Girl Scouts who want to get out of the snow and down the mountain."

Nick asked, "How many girls are there?"

"Seven," replied Jeane.

"Okay," said Nick, "if I put your packs on top, I can get all of you in the station wagon."

Jeane ran back yelling, "Hurry! We've got a ride to the Visitor's Center!"

When we got to the Center the girls headed for the heaters to dry their clothes and get warm. Jeane carefully removed the tape. I asked the ranger if he'd heard anything about the other group. He hadn't, which meant they were still up on the mountain. But where? Asking several questions about their supplies and the number of people in the group, the ranger advised waiting until morning to start a search. I called Mr. Valentine to bring the car. I dropped the girls in Gatlinburg and took him back to the motel.

My mind was on searching for Barbara's group. The only way would be on foot, hiking the trail from Cosby Knob Campground. I hoped I didn't find the girls clumped together frozen to death, or one of them with a broken leg. The Smoky Mountain National Park is huge; it might take days to find them if they stumbled off the trail. "Oh! Don't let me think such thoughts. Think positive," I admonished myself.

A car behind me was blinking its lights and followed me into the motel lot. Before I knew what was happening, Diane was hugging me and tears were flowing. Barbara's group was in the car. Jamie asked, "Where are the girls?"

38

I assured them that they were fine and in Gatlinburg. I asked Barbara, "Where did we miss you?"

Barbara replied, "Your group must have passed when we went the quarter mile back to Peck Corner Lean-to for lunch. We came down the trail at Cosby Campground, and the ranger brought us to the motel to pick up your car."

As we drove back into Gatlinburg we saw my girls walking to Baskin-Robbins. Everyone began to yell and squeal as the girls ran to greet their friends. What excitement! Through hugs, tears and laughter, questions flew faster than they could be answered. I was limp with relief and felt His guiding hand had been with us. We continued our boisterous reunion in a restaurant.

"It was almost dark, and we were still hiking, when we saw this big black thing," Lisa said, her eyes shining with excitement. "Mom stopped and gasped, 'Is that a bear?' Terri and I thought it looked like one too, so we started yelling and making noises, but the bear didn't move. Then we threw rocks at it, and the bear still didn't move. Finally we started walking toward the bear. The bear turned out to be just a big rock, but it sure had us fooled."

Jamie chimed in, "We kept hearing a funny, clanking noise as we walked down the mountain. Mary figured out that it was our frozen pantlegs hitting together as we walked."

Jeane told of taping her legs and added, "When we came to Charlie's Bunion I thought I was a goner. If Sharon hadn't grabbed my hand, I think the wind would have blown me off the mountain."

"We didn't waste any time there either," Diane added. "The wind was blowing so hard it was tough to brace ourselves against it."

Still buzzing, we spent the night at Laurel Springs Motel. When we woke, Barbara and I followed the snow plow to Mt. Collins where she'd left her car. She told me what had happened with her group. "The first night two people were in the Mt. Collins shelter. They had a fire going when we got there, but it rained during the night. The shelter leaked, and Terri's sleeping bag got wet, so she had to crawl in with Lisa to keep warm."

"Did the sleeping bag get wet enough to add to its weight?" I asked.

"No, but it never dried out," she answered. "The next day we walked in a misting rain. When we reached Ice Water Springs Shelter we found that it faced north and the wind was blowing at gale speed right into the shelter. We spread our ponchos across the front but even that didn't help. The people who were already at the shelter had a fire going in the fireplace, but it was freezing cold. Back on the trail in the morning, Terri started having pains in her chest.

I told her to button her jacket and put on a hat, but she didn't seem to understand."

"Do you know about hypothermia?" I interrupted.

"No. What's that?"

I explained it to her. "Do you think Terri might have been in the early stages of it? One of the symptoms is general listlessness."

"Maybe," said Barbara. "The wind was really cold. It was handy, though, to have icicles to suck when we were thirsty; it kept us from having to get out our canteens."

"That's another reason Terri could have hypothermia," I said. "Eating something frozen slows down your body functions even faster."

"Well," Barbara continued, "we just had to get out of the wind to eat, and when we reached the sign to Peck's Corner Lean-to, we walked back to the shelter, not thinking that you might pass while we were off the trail."

"After lunch," she continued, "Terri kept getting slower and slower. Finally, Lisa and I took her pack and carried it between us. It was getting dark and we weren't to Tri-Corner Knob Shelter. Lisa and I had to lead Terri and feel our way the last mile in the dark, since I'd given Susan my flashlight. Diane and Jamie were starting back to meet us when we arrived. We found no dry wood, so we tried to use the sterno to start a fire, but no luck. We ate our gorp, lukewarm chocolate and leftover peanut butter crackers."

"Did Lisa and Terri sleep in the same sleeping bag again?" I asked.

"Yes," Barbara said, "Terri's bag was still wet."

"That's good," I said. "One of the first aid treatments for hypothermia is to put the victim into a sleeping bag with another person."

"I woke up in the night with diarrhea, probably because I'd been eating icicles—another good reason for not doing that!" Barbara laughed. "I also had blisters on my heels the size of quarters. I was miserable; I thought morning would never come! At daylight I decided we'd better get down from the mountain, so I put it to a vote. Everyone was in favor but Diane. She said, 'My mother would want us to finish what we started and wouldn't stop because of the snow.' I told her I wasn't her mother, but I was sure if Mama Boots realized how sick Terri and I were, she'd want us to come down."

I laughed. Diane knew her mother pretty well—the "do-or-die lady." She didn't know I was trying to get off the mountain too.

Barbara continued, "I convinced Diane that for the safety of the group, we should go down the trail to Cosby Campground. I'd put on my tennis shoes and turned the heels down so they wouldn't rub my blisters, but they still hurt. At the camp ground a ranger put all seven of us and our packs in his car and took us to Laurel Springs Motel where you'd left your car. No one was at the motel, and your car was gone, so the ranger agreed to drive us to Gatlinburg. On the way, Diane shouted, 'There's Mom's car, going the other way, and Mom is driving it!' The ranger turned around and followed, but you didn't stop 'til you got to the motel."

"I'm glad you came down, Barbara," I said as I pulled up beside her parked car, "I wouldn't have been able to drive to Davenport Gap in this snow."

Barbara walked to her car, laughing. "Mother always told me that God takes care of fools and babies. I don't know which we are, but He really came through."

We returned to pick up the girls and started home. All things considered—sore muscles and bruised spirits—this trip was superb and would have lasting effects.

*　　*　　*　　*　　*

After what could have been a tragedy in the Smoky Mountains, I was having second thoughts about continuing to offer my volunteer service as a backpacking consultant. Being in charge of the safety of teenage girls on a backpack trip is a sizable responsibility.

I still wanted to hike the A.T. and to give John and Diane the self-confidence and appreciation for the wilderness that comes with hiking the Trail. We planned a family hiking vacation to the Pedlar District of the George Washington National Forest in Virginia. We would hike seventy-two miles starting at US 501 at the James River, north to Rockfish Gap at I-64.

At our last Scout meeting for the year, the girls were discussing summer plans. "I'd like to go backpacking," Sharon said. "I don't have anything planned for the summer."

Before I realized it, I was telling her about the family trip we had planned. Sharon jumped with excitement. "Mama Boots, can I please go along. I won't take up much room. Please, please! You said Martha wasn't going because she was teaching swimming lessons. I can take her place. Oh, please!"

Sharon's enthusiasm made it impossible to say no. Then I thought, we still have room for one more in the car. I'll call Lisa. "Oh yes, I'd love to go. I can't wait," said Lisa.

On August 7, the six of us started hiking on a well-graded trail that followed a small creek, then started ascending steeply to the crest of the Blue

Ridge at Fuller Rocks. As we hiked the long switchbacks and over rock outcroppings, the hot August sun throbbed unbearably. Our water supply was low, and our clothes dripped with sweat. Fortunately there were plenty of big juicy blackberries. About four in the afternoon we came to a gravel road leading to Bluff Mountain fire tower. Diane asked, "Can we climb up the steps?"

"That's a good idea," I said. "Let's pick some of these berries and climb up to rest for a while."

The cool breeze was refreshing, and the berries quenched our thirst and restored our energy. Lisa asked, "Is that the James River way down there? It looks like a little creek. How far down is it?"

"According to the guidebook, the altitude at the James River is 750 feet. That's about the same as Jefferson County Forest back home," I said. "The altitude of Bluff Mountain is 3,372 feet. We've climbed over 2,600 feet. No wonder we're puffing so hard."

For the next few days the Trail led around Pedlar Lake, near the Blue Ridge Parkway, with glimpses of Bluff Mountain. On top of Bald Mountain Sharon remarked, "How come this is called Bald Mountain? It isn't bald! Shrubs and trees are growing here!"

"It must have been bald when the mountain was named," I answered. "Over the years the wind and birds probably carried the seeds here."

When we reached Cole Mountain, she noted, "Now this mountain is a bald, no trees, just grass and rocks."

"This mountain has been cleared by man for the microwave equipment," I told her.

While we ate lunch on the bald, it started raining. Sharon and Diane stuck out their tongues trying to catch the raindrops and sang:

> If all of the rain drops were lemon drops and gum drops, oh what a rain that would be. I wouldn't mind if the sun never shined; I'd stand outside with my mouth open wide. If all of the rain drops were lemon drops and gum drops, oh what a rain that would be.

Three boys came along and gave us a strange look. They must have wondered about our sanity, but they were lost and couldn't find the trail down the mountain. Although appearing a little doubtful when Sharon and Diane offered to escort them to the trail, they followed the girls. When the girls returned, Sharon looked around pensively and said, "They must call these

42

mountains Blue Ridge Mountains because they're wrapped in a snug, blue haze."

"I wonder if it's this hazy when it isn't raining," Lisa responded.

Later we came to a huge rock outcropping. Lisa looked up and asked, "Do we have to climb that?"

Then she noticed the white blazes going up the side of the rock. Diane put her fingers in an open place in the rock, and Sharon said, "There's a place to put your foot over to the right."

Diane carefully put her right foot in the spot, then looked around to find another place to put her other hand. Lisa said, "To your left looks like a good spot."

Diane inched her way up the side of the rock with Sharon and Lisa right behind. Reaching a level spot, they turned around and gave directions to Papa and me. John, the sure-footed one, was already on the pinnacle. Rock climbing was new, but we met the challenge and felt satisfaction at mastering the big rocks.

At night we bathed in mountain streams. By day we climbed over rock outcroppings and grassy areas with the Blue Ridge Mountains always in sight. Curious about the names of the mountains, I retrieved the guidebook and found it was the "Religious Range." We would be hiking on "The Priest" before the day was over.

From the summit of "The Priest," we could see the Tye River Valley, 3,000 feet below. Descending the switchbacks, we crossed the bridge over the Tye River on our way to Harpers Creek Lean-to. We shared the lean-to with Phillip and Joane Hobart, members of the Tidewater Appalachian Trail Club. They were out on the trail refurbishing the white-painted blazes. This meeting with volunteers who maintain the trail gave us a chance to tell them how much we appreciated their work.

Thursday we started the climb up Three Ridges, the mountain we had seen from the other side of the Tye River. When I neared the top I found Diane and Lisa talking to the Pearson family from Ohio. They were hiking the A.T. in short sections on weekends and vacations. After a short visit we continued on, and the girls came upon an ideal place to eat lunch on an out cropping. By the time I caught up, Sharon was describing the view. She pointed and said, "I bet that's Three Ridges. It's the closest and it's a ridge with three humps."

Lisa pointed, "That must be the Tye River Valley."

Diane interrupted, "That mountain way over there must be 'The Priest.'"

I questioned, "Do you think we can see the microwave equipment on Cole Mountain from here?"

We had hiked on all these mountains. We cheered like a team that had just won a game and felt we had established "bragger's rights."

Warmed by the early morning sun, we acted like mountain goats climbing in and out between the rock on Humpback Mountain. At open places we could look down to the Blue Ridge Parkway winding through the mountains. From an outcropping, the view was 360 degrees, extending from the southern end of the Shenandoah National Park, all the way back to the Tye River Valley. We didn't want the backpack trip to end. It had been a great accomplishment and had given us enormous self-confidence. I will never forget the pride on the girl's faces. My enthusiasm for hiking the A.T. with Girl Scouts had been revived. I knew I would soon be backpacking somewhere on the A.T. with my young friends.

Waiting for Papa to return with the car, I asked, "Would you like to read in the guidebook and find an interesting place to hike next summer?"

Lisa read about the rhododendron near the top of Mt. Rogers. Sharon said, "I'd like to see that."

Lisa added, "I bet my mother would like to hike there, and she could help with transportation."

"Let's work on that for next June," I suggested.

CHAPTER SIX

The news of a June backpack trip spread to four troops. By the time we were ready to purchase and repack food, there were thirteen girls in the group. Barbara, Mrs. McWilliams and I drove the group to Damascus, Virginia, for a forty-seven mile trek north to the small town of Teas, Virginia. It was about five o'clock in the afternoon when we began to hike.

We made camp before dark and everyone was on the trail by six-thirty A.M.. We'd hiked about an hour when we came to a portion of ungraded trail that was muddy and slick. Sharon asked, "What happened to the nice trail? I keep sliding off of this."

I explained, "The trail has been recently detoured away from private property. There's a NO TRESPASSING sign over there where the trail used to go."

By lunch we reached the end of the ungraded trail and stopped at Fox Creek, a large stream and favorite resting spot for hikers. Crossing Fox Creek after lunch, Karen P. warned, "Be careful not to fall in the creek. You'll get your socks wet and get blisters." No sooner said than done, she slipped into the creek. Laurie slipped and stepped backwards, landing feet and all in the water. Everyone had trouble crossing on the rocks.

We pitched our tents by a small bridge. Two boys, Rick and Tim, camped on the other side. Gleefully the girls spent the evening going back and forth with samples of freeze-dried peas and instant pudding. The bridge was very old with many missing boards, making it great sport to balance the food and themselves without falling into the creek. Rick and Tim had M & M's and cookies which they exchanged, unwillingly, for our food.

Refreshed by a good night's sleep, we found ourselves on an almost vertical trail with large rocks and muddy holes made by grazing cattle. This stretch of the Trail, on private land, was still not graded, making it very rough. Alice and Lynn K. were puffing up the steep mountain when Alice started swatting at the bugs. She fussed, "Go away bugs. Bite someone else. I'm having enough trouble getting up this mountain without mosquitoes and flies biting me."

"Let's stop and put on some insect repellent," I encouraged.

Lynn K. said, "This stuff sure stinks!"

"It's better than being eaten by the bugs," Alice replied.

Alice, Lynn K. and I came to the bottom of the bald and looked up. We could see Patty and Karen sitting on a huge rock near the top of the mountain. Alice remarked, "Patty and Karen look like a couple of buzzards sitting up there, waiting to see if we make it. Maybe that's why it's called Buzzard's Rock."

When we reached the top, the girls had a pleasant surprise—a cool breeze and an extended view of mountains for miles. Suzanne remarked, "I feel so small when I look at the mountains. At the same time, I feel really strong to have gotten here on my own two feet."

Patty added, "Backpacking does give you mixed feelings. When I reach the top I'm hot, disgusted and in pain, but after resting and watching the clouds floating over the distant mountains, I forget all about that and I'm ready to do it all over again."

In a gentle breeze, we walked across White Top Mountain. Sharon, Laurie and I waited at Elk Garden parking lot, for Barbara and Mrs. McWilliams to bring our additional supplies of food and to hike with us for two days. They would get off the trail after Rhododendron Gap, to get the cars and meet us in Teas at the end of our trek. By having food brought to us midway, we eliminated considerable weight in our packs at the beginning of our hike. Distributing the food between our packs, we headed for Deep Gap Shelter where our group planned to spend the night.

It was early when we started the long climb up Mt. Rogers, the highest peak in Virginia at 5,729 feet. Red Spruce and Fraser Fir trees covered the top. The forest floor had a spongy texture because it was in the clouds most of the time.

We left the top of the mountain and came to a bald area with our vista of the mountains returning. Diane, Lynn B. and Lisa, our fast hikers, were ready to leave by the time Suzanne, Carol, Patty, Janet, and Sharon reached the big rock outcropping. Janet held Carol's hand, so she wouldn't fall as she climbed up the rock. From the top, fifty feet above the Trail, the girls were spellbound by the sight of thousands of rhododendron bushes covering hundreds of acres. The bushes in full bloom ranged in color from pink to deep purple. Sharon remarked, "This is indescribable. The entire ridge has a purple glow. There's no end to the blooms."

Carol added, "Look way over there on that ridge. You can still see pink bushes."

When Alice, Lynn K. and Martha, the last of the group, reached the top of the rock, they noticed Diane's red pack starting across the bald ridge and sang loudly, "Tongo." Diane responded, "Tongo." We all joined in and filled the air with the Girl Scout echo song.

Coming down from the rock, we walked through the rhododendron. At Old Orchard Shelter we sat around the campfire talking about the day's events. "Do you like backpacking?" I asked Patty.

"Yes," she replied. "I like the way everyone shares in the planning and preparations and all the tasks on the hike. It also gives me a feeling of independence. I'm really impressed with what I can do."

"You really can see the balance of nature—all those flowers blooming like a highly cultivated garden, but with no help from anyone except nature," Suzanne commented.

"The rhododendron made me feel closer to God," Sharon remarked.

Before going to bed, Alice and Lynn K. asked Laurie for their share of breakfast, so they could get an early start. Alice and Lynn were always the last ones to arrive at all our stops and had been teased about being c.t.'s (cow tails). They were determined not to be the c.t.'s today. We lunched together at Comer Falls, and the competition was on to be the first to get to the lean-to. Lisa and Alice won the race, but the rest of the trekkers were close behind.

Sitting around our last campfire of the trip, some of the girls decided to write a will to give to future hikers.

Alice leaves her pants to fry on the grill.
Lynn K. leaves her c.t. to a slow hiker.
Janet B. leaves her Vienna Sausage to anyone.
Lynn B. leaves her shoulder pads to the latrine.
Suzanne leaves her tan to someone who burns.
Patty leaves her mustard sardines to the hungry.

Karen leaves her songs to someone who can't sing.
Laurie leaves her unusual dance to a school of dancing.
Lisa leaves her speedy legs to slow hikers.
Diane leaves her cooking skill to those who need it.
Sharon leaves the log for someone else to write.

*   *   *   *   *

M.S., who had been on several hikes, and her troop wanted to hike Rhododendron Gap in June. We spent the night at the hostel in Damascus. Damascus is a friendly town which is popular with hikers and encircled by mountains. One of the churches furnishes an old house with a stove and refrigerator for hikers while they pick up mail and restock food supplies.

On our first day out, we discovered a rerouting away from Taylor Valley. After passage of the National Scenic Trail Act in 1968, an Act of Congress making the A.T. a protected wilderness trail, it became necessary for trail clubs to reroute away from towns, roads and private property. The guidebooks could not keep up with the changes, and we had no information about the rerouting.

The Trail turned and started up a mountain. Late in the afternoon, Lisa L. and Tina insisted that we stay on the old trail, but M.S. and I felt we should follow the rerouting. Winding our way up seventeen switchbacks, Tina asked, "Why are we going back and forth across the mountain? It would be quicker just to go straight up."

"If all hikers went straight up," I explained, "it would create a drainage ditch for rain run-off, and the water would take topsoil with it. The Mount Rogers Trail Club worked hard to make the switchbacks so the rain can soak into the ground instead of creating an erosion problem."

We were ready to stop for the night when we reached the top. While searching for water, I saw an unusually bright-pink mountain laurel bush. Normally they are white, but this bush was in full sun. It made me think of the story of Moses and the burning bush in the Bible. I wondered if this might have been the kind of bush he saw. My second thought was, "Lord, we don't really need the Ten Commandments right now, but we sure could use some water!" In a short time, M.S. called to me saying she had found a small spring with enough water for cooking.

After breakfast M.S. said, "Mama Boots, let's leave the girls to finish packing and find a creek to brush our teeth and wash."

M.S. and I soon came to a creek with plenty of clear water. When the girls caught up, Tina asked, "Is there time for us to splash around in the creek?"

M.S. stated, "It's still early. Why not? Have fun!"

The girls cavorted about in the creek, doing ballet dance steps, prancing around splashing water and having fun. After a while, M.S. said, "Mama Boots, why don't we start hiking. Maybe the girls will get out of the water and come on."

The girls caught up at lunch and told us all about the fun they'd had in the creek. Crossing several roads and following an old forest service road, we camped that evening by a rickety old bridge.

Next morning we were ready for Buzzard's Rock. As we started the climb, Crystal asked, "Why is this mountain so steep? It doesn't have switchbacks like the ones we just came over."

"This is private land," I said. "See the cows over there? It'll be graded after the final agreement is made with the owner."

I reached the top and sat, like a buzzard, looking back down the mountain. The girls were working hard to make the difficult climb. They were impressed by their accomplishment when they reached the top and looked back on what they had done.

Three boys we had met at the hostel in Damascus, Bob, Bill, and Dave, were at Deep Gap shelter. The boys had taken the old trail through Taylor Valley. M.S. laughed, "Now I know why the girls wanted to take the old trail."

"Yes," Cindy added, "and we had that hard, steep climb to make it up the mountain and had very little water."

Everyone giggled as Susan told about seeing a nude man walking around in the woods. We hoped he didn't get too many scratches as he ran away when he heard us on the trail.

As we climbed up Mt. Rogers, the rain subsided and soon M.S. and I reached Rhododendron Gap. The rhododendron glistened with little drops of water on their petals. Paula said, "Karen, your description didn't do this justice. It's a zillion times more beautiful!"

Reluctant to leave, I sat on the big rock and watched the girls as they continued hiking across the ridge. When I came to the lean-to M.S. said, "The girls have gone on. They want to camp by the creek."

Our water lovers played in the creek until almost dark and still had the energy to manage an evening of singing with Bob, Bill, and Dave.

Leaving camp around eight A.M., M.S. and I moseyed along having a good time talking about all the Girl Scout activities we were involved in. When I

looked up, I saw a yellow blaze and said, "Oh, my gosh! We're following the wrong trail."

M.S. gasped, "I wonder how long we've been following this trail? I wonder where the girls are?"

We picked up the pace, and soon we were back to the white blazes of the A.T.. M.S. questioned, "Do you think the girls are ahead of us?"

I remarked, "Knowing them, they're probably playing in a creek somewhere."

It wasn't long before we heard laughter and splashing water. "I think we've found our water ladies," I laughed. "They must be at Comer's Falls. It's located in a gorge with a sizable drop and a series of cascades, a perfect setting for lots of fun."

Tina said, "Cindy and I were first to get our shoes off. Paula and Crystal were right behind, and soon everyone was in the water."

Crystal said, "The water here is fun because it's moving so fast over the rocks."

They had a delightful time playing the afternoon away until M.S. finally had to say, "Girls we have to get to the shelter before nightfall."

At one time or another during the day, everyone strayed off the trail. M.S. and I had been at the shelter for an hour, and there was no sign of Karen, Paula, and Susan. M.S. said, "If they aren't here in fifteen minutes, we'd better look for them."

About ten minutes later we were relieved to hear giggling in the distance. Karen burst out, "We missed the sign to the lean-to and hiked a long time before we realized it."

After supper we scoured the cooking pots for our next trip and chatted. Everyone agreed that living without tap water could be fun when there were so many lovely waterfalls. Cindy said, "Someday I'd like to hike the Trail all in one summer. I could probably do it if I didn't stop to play in the water so much."

CHAPTER SEVEN

The girls wanted to try a new challenge. We'd battled April snow on the trail, so why not a post-Christmas hike in Georgia? We'd need more equipment, warmer sleeping bags, and insolite, a non-conducting material, to protect us from the cold ground. My family had given me a backpack tent and down sleeping bag, for which I was especially grateful, and Margaret H., a girl who'd gone on our first hike, also had a tent. This gave us room to sleep six.

The day after Christmas, we drove to Amicalola Falls, Georgia and started hiking the approach trail to the top of Springer Mountain, the southern terminus of the Trail. Darkness came before we reached the top. Groping along with flashlights, we came to Springer Mountain Lean-to and found it was full. We had the dubious pleasure of pitching our tents in a brisk wind in the dark. We thought surely the tents would blow away before we got them staked down.

Diane and Mary, a Scout from Troop 116, and I crawled into our down sleeping bags in my new tent. Diane and Mary were the only Girl Scouts in the group. The parents of the others were reluctant to let them go at this time of year, but Mary had hiked with us on numerous occasions, including the snowy trip in the Smokies, and was eager to try more winter backpacking. Margaret and Martha, college students, and Molly, now a student nurse, were in the other tent.

Wind whipping our tents made sleeping difficult, but morning brought a bright, crisp day which was perfect for hiking. The trail was easy until we came to Hawk Mountain. Hawk Mountain Lean-to was surrounded by ice. Dorothy, Doug, Vista and Charles, whom we'd met at Springer Mountain Lean-to, found an old army barracks which they invited us to share with them. Though abandoned for years, it was dry and comfortable.

Morning dawned on another crisp day. It took the skills of gymnasts to balance ourselves on the logs that crossed some of the fast-running streams and to hop from rock to rock across others. Diane and Mary stopped by a waterfall to rest in the sun. "This can't be December. It's not cold enough," said Mary. "I was cold last night, but it sure is nice now."

"This sure is a different way to spend Christmas vacation," Diane added. "It's fun to sit and watch the water washing over the rocks. We'll have to tell the other girls how nice it is to hike this time of year."

Unable to find a level place to pitch our tents at Gooch Gap Lean-to, we spent the night trying to keep from rolling down the mountain.

After less than an hour on the trail, the rain started. We planned to hike 11-9/10 miles. Climbing switchback after switchback, we reached the top of Blood Mountain, the highest point in Georgia. A crowd had already gathered in the old, two-room cabin. More and more hikers emerged from the woods until Blood Mountain Cabin looked like Grand Central Station. Rain still came down in blinding sheets, and we found that the old building leaked. It looked like a logging camp. People were stretched in all directions—some on tables, some under tables, some crossways on the floor. Everyone was trying to avoid getting wet.

Like islands, the mountain tops emerged in a sea of clouds, tinged pink by the early morning sun. We sat and marveled at the view. One hiker said it made her think of cotton candy, another thought of a giant dish of ice cream with chocolate cookies in the middle. I asked my group, "Why do you keep coming back to hike on the Trail?"

Mary replied, "I really can't explain it. My emotions vary from one extreme to another. On bad days with steep climbs, cold rain, and my back, shoulders and feet hurting, I question why I'm spending my holidays doing this. But then there's the peaceful contented feelings, laughing and singing favorite songs with friends, and the incredible scenery along the way. Those things outweigh the discomforts and pain."

Diane added, "Like now. Here we are admiring this early morning scene with Mike and George who we met at the cabin last night."

Mary continued, "It's always exciting to get to the lean-to and meet new friends, share hiking stories and cooking fires. After a good nights sleep, which I always have because I'm exhausted at the end of the day, I'm ready to go again. At the end of a hike, I can't wait to get to school and brag to my friends. It's quite an accomplishment to backpack, especially in December and April."

*   *   *   *   *

Post-Christmas hiking was an exciting adventure for Senior Scouts. Papa was going to accompany us, but his doctor discovered a serious back problem and told him, "If you slip, and your back goes out, the only way your wife will be able to get you out of the woods will be on a stretcher." Papa and I decided it would be best for him to give up backpacking. He could be our moral support, a contact person and our number one fan. John took time off from work to help with the driving. John didn't really like backpacking but had logged 200 miles on the Trail.

Marty W., a Senior Planning Board Advisor, and her group of girls planned to begin at Dicks Creek Gap and go south. My group would get on the Trail at Neels Gap and hike north, providing a car at both ends of the trek. Janet found a water faucet where we filled our canteens. Walking a short distance in the clouds, we made camp in the rain. Water ran down the sloping ground to wet everything in our tents. The pants Kathy was going to wear were soaked. At dawn I saw her heading down the hill, still in her sweats, and asked, "Where are you going?"

She replied, "To the car to get my dry pants."

"In fifteen minutes, your dry pants will be as wet as these, and then you won't have any dry pants to wear at the end of the hike," I cautioned her.

"Eek, Oh, Burr!" came from the tent as she put on the cool, wet pants. Fortunately, the temperature was in the mid-fifties with very little wind, so there was no danger of hypothermia. Shaking some of the water off our tents, we packed and start hiking.

The Trail began with a gradual grade, but soon became steep. At the top of Levelland Mountain we could hardly see six feet in front of us. As we entered Tesnatee Gap, Mary sniffed the air. "Is that smoke I smell? Someone must have a fire going. Is there a lean-to near here?"

Diane chimed in, "It smells like someone is cooking. Let's hurry! Maybe we can dry our pants by the fire."

Two men were cooking game hen at the lean-to, and they invited us to have a taste when the delicacy was finished. We gratefully accepted, drying our pantlegs by the fire as we waited. Janet remarked, "This is the first time I've eaten game hen cooked like this. It sure has a yummy taste."

Mary asked, "Why don't we try this sometime on a camping trip?"

Diane suggested, "It wouldn't do on a backpack trip. It would have to be kept cold and would be bulky to carry in our packs."

After hiking eleven miles in the rain, we found Low Gap Lean-to was full. Diane and Mary pitched the tents while Kathy built a fire to dry our sleeping bags. I lit the backpack stove and Janet, the cook for the evening, prepared our supper. The moon was shining, but an hour after crawling into our sleeping bags, we heard rain.

At daylight, I asked Janet, "What do you think of the idea of eating a cold breakfast, packing up and heading for the next lean-to. We could dry out our clothes there before we continue hiking."

"That's a good idea," she agreed. We woke the others and had Pop Tarts and Tang before heading for the next lean-to.

Squishing along in the pouring rain on an old service road, we reached the top of Horsetrough Mountain, descended into Chattahoochee Gap, and came to Rocky Knob Lean-to by noon. Kathy soon had a fire going and Diane prepared the oats, adding raisins and brown sugar as she cooked them. Sitting by the warm fire, Sharon said, "These oats are delicious; they sure hit the spot."

Kathy added, "I don't usually like oats, but these are really good. Maybe it's because I'm cold, wet and hungry."

Janet, Cindy and Mary put the sleeping bags by the fire while Kathy, Diane and Mickie spread the tents to dry. It had quit raining, but the dampness and clouds remained. Since Marty's group planned to camp at Rocky Knob, we decided to stay and have a fun night visiting. John and I put up a tent to leave room for the other group in the lean-to. Around four o'clock, a group of boys came by. They had a message from Marty: "If you see a group of girls, tell them Marty's not feeling well. We're going to the campground at Unicoi Gap and get off the trail in the morning."

Janet said, "Let's start early and get there before they leave tomorrow."

Cindy and Kathy liked the idea, so they packed up the tents and the clothes drying by the fire. At the crack of dawn, Cindy, Kathy and Janet were up and packing while Diane, Mary and Mickie fixed breakfast. John and I were taking our tent down as the girls left. John said, "Hurry Mom. I want to catch the girls," and left while I was packing the pots and stove.

Walking back to the campground, I found the girls. "Where's John?" I asked. Nobody had seen him. He must have missed the note Marty left on a tree, and he didn't know the campground was a tenth of a mile off the trail.

"Lisa," I asked, "Where's Marty?"

"She and Jeane have gone to Neels Gap to get your car and take it to Dicks Creek Gap. We're going home," she informed me.

Allowing the girls to visit as long as possible, I finally said, "Girls we have to leave and try to catch John before he thinks we're lost and sends out a search party."

I feared my group might say something about quitting because it was still misting rain. Their clothes, boots, and socks were soaked, but I didn't hear the first complaint. They were an extremely determined group.

From Unicoi Gap it was a gradual 1000 foot climb to the summit of Rocky Mountain. We moved right along, but by lunch time we still hadn't caught John. He must almost be to the lean-to and thinking the girls had wings to have gotten that far ahead of him.

John was waiting at the sign to the Montray Lean-to. He said in a panicky voice, "Where are the girls? I never did catch them. I've been waiting for hours."

I told him, "They're right behind me."

He said "Did they get lost? I never passed them."

I explained the totally confusing day to him, and he laughed with relief, glad we were all together.

The lean-to was full, but the people had a fire and let us cook our supper in the shelter. It was our last night on the trail, and we were eleven miles away from the car. We had planned to be home on New Year's Eve, but it looked as though we would be spending New Year's Eve in a motel.

I woke the group at dawn. We raced over several ridges and into gaps with only a few hundred feet elevation change to get out of the rain we had sloshed through for four days. At a motel in Murphy, North Carolina, we all agreed it felt good to don dry clothes.

*   *   *   *   *

Another group of girls wanted to hike Georgia in December. Two carloads traveled to Dicks Creek Gap, where we camped for the night. On the first day, with snow on the ground, we hiked against a cold north wind. Fresh snow started to fall before we reached the A-frame Muskrat Creek Shelter. During the night another three inches fell. For the sake of health and safety, we agreed to abort the trip. Next time we could be better prepared.

The next December we took up the challenge again. Six of us prepared to start at Wallace Gap and go south to Dicks Creek Gap. When we reached Rock Gap Lean-to in the early afternoon, Shrimp (Patricia H.) shivered, "Do you think we could build a fire and have something hot to drink? I'm really cold."

Shrimp and Michelle quickly had a fire going, and we had hot spiced tea with our sack suppers. By six-thirty the wind was blowing hard. We gave up trying to keep warm by the fire and crawled into our sleeping bags. The temperature was only sixteen degrees Fahrenheit, and the three-sided lean-to didn't offer much protection. The rain fly we put across the front helped block some of the wind and darkened the inside of the lean-to. We fell asleep exhausted.

We were relieved to find that no one had frozen during the night. It was still cold and windy, but the sun was bright, and Michelle couldn't pass up climbing the fire tower on Alberts Mountain. She was a girl who wanted to see, hear and get involved in everything. It would take more than a little wind to stop her. Up the steps right behind Michelle was Peggy G., a witty, easy going girl who never got upset about anything. "My cat, Ralph, would have better sense than to climb up a fire tower in this stiff wind," she said.

Shrimp and the rest of us followed along a bit less enthusiastically, but the view from the top made the climb worthwhile. The silver grays of bare branches flickered among the black and brown trunks of oaks and evergreens. The forest floor was a carpet of variegated brown leaves rustling in the wind, protecting wildflowers which waited patiently for spring.

We descended the south side of the mountain and arrived at Betty Creek Gap. Here we found a clump of rhododendron that would help block our tents from the wind. By the time Michelle and I had supper ready, everyone was almost too cold to eat. After a few bites, we snuggled into sleeping bags and were asleep before dark. Though Michelle had a down bag, she woke up cold and climbed in with Shrimp, putting her own bag on top of them. By daylight we'd been in our sleeping bags for more than twelve hours and emerged to find the water in our canteens frozen. "Can we use water from Betty Creek to fix breakfast?" asked Shrimp.

"Yes, " I replied, "if we use the water purification tablets."

We had a hot breakfast, packed our gear and were on the Trail. Exertion would help keep us warm, but the wind drew tears from our eyes as we hiked the switchbacks. Despite our discomfort, we enjoyed seeing small streams rushing down the mountain—a view not possible except in winter when the trees are bare.

When Peggy and Shrimp reached Beech Gap, Shrimp spotted a small fire circle and said, "Let's camp here." Pam and Peggy built a fire in the fireplace to dry the body moisture from our sleeping bags. As they pitched their tents, the girls noticed a ball of ice in one tent. "How'd that get there?" asked Michelle.

"Beats me," said Shrimp. "I didn't put it there."

"It's condensation," I explained. "It formed and froze on the inside of the tent while you slept. You've been carrying it all day."

We ate quickly and again were in our sleeping bags before dark. The wind whipped the flies of our tents which made me wonder if it might snow.

We woke to clear skies, but the wind was still blowing. Eagerly, we started the long climb up Standing Indian. The panorama from the top was colossal and endless. The rock-entrenched Tallulah Gorge and Southern Appalachian Mountains stretched before us, and the wind blew at such velocity that Peggy said, "I feel like I could soar. Looking back at what I've done the past few days is an exhilarating and powerful feeling. It makes me want to keep hiking just to see what the next ten or twenty miles will bring."

Our stay here was brief, since it was a long way to White Oak Gap. Hiking along, we came to a frozen waterfall blocking the trail. "Oh my gosh!" Peggy exclaimed. "We're never going to get around this."

I gasped, "We've come more than halfway. Let's see if we can find a way. Pick up a stick to help keep your balance, and scoot your feet across the ice."

Michelle said, "I'll try anything once," and started inching her way around the ice. The rest of us followed and were soon starting the descent to Deep Gap. The A-frame Muskrat Lean-to was becoming a dear friend. It had sheltered us from a thunderstorm in April, a snowstorm the previous December, and on this night, offered cozy shelter from winter wind. Located behind a clump of rhododendron, it's hardly visible until you are there. The six of us snuggled into the back of the shelter and sang a few songs before falling asleep. Michelle and Shrimp had trouble getting comfortable in the same bag and woke me. Giving Michelle my wool pants and shirt, she was soon warm and asleep in her own sleeping bag.

An inch of snow fell during the night. While the temperature was warmer, the snow was wet and the clouds were low and dripping. On an open ridge on the Georgia-North Carolina border, Michelle spotted a deformed tree. "What a funny shape," she said, "It looks like antlers of a giant reindeer. I wonder what caused it to have that shape?"

"You'd be deformed too," Shrimp said, "if you'd been whipped by this wind all the time."

We hurried on into Georgia, not stopping for lunch until we reached Plum Orchard Lean-to. Michelle said, "It's only one-thirty. Why don't we go on to Dicks Creek Gap? We're awfully close."

"It won't do any good," I answered. "Papa won't be there to pick us up until tomorrow."

"Start the stove, Michelle, and I'll get water for hot spiced tea," said Shrimp. "We'll drink it with the rest of our food."

We got into our sleeping bags, laughing and talking about how cold we'd been earlier in the day. We sang and ate all afternoon. The weather was miserable, but we were snug.

On New Year's Eve morning we made a fast trip to Dicks Creek Gap where Papa was waiting. "Michelle and I tried to sleep in the same bag," Shrimp said to Papa.

"That must have been cozy," said Papa. "Were you warm that way?"

"No," Michelle chimed in, "I was freezing the whole time until Mama Boots gave me her wool shirt and pants."

Shrimp told about the wind almost blowing her off Standing Indian and Peggy said, "I could have stood there all day, no matter how cold I got. The view and wind made me feel like I was on top of the world."

"It would have been easy to just give up when we came to that ice on the trail," Michelle added, "but I'm glad we didn't. Now I'm confident that I can do anything I want to."

Peggy added, "I wondered what I'd gotten into when we came to that frozen waterfall. I thought sure I'd die or break a leg!"

Pam told about the temperature—twenty degrees during the day, with a wind chill of zero. Having survived and solved the problems caused by the cold, the girls were intoxicated with pride.

*   *   *   *   *

It was time to try another April trip. We planned to start at Wallace Gap, North Carolina and hike north to Fontana Dam at the southern end of the Smokies, a fifty-five mile hike.

We began the easy climb in sunshine. It was great to be on the trail after a long winter. The fresh mountain air and warm sun cured our cabin fever. The girls, finding a grassy spot, reclined in the sun to relax and watch the fluffy clouds drifting in the bright blue sky.

Shortly after we left our campsite, rain set in, and by the time we reached the top of Wayah Bald, we were in clouds. A memorial tower had been placed on this mountain, honoring John B. Byrne, a former supervisor of the Nantahala National Forest. We climbed the tower, but we couldn't see two feet.

Inside the tower, Diane and Mary found a dry place for lunch. As we were finishing, two girls and two boys came in and rudely asked us to leave. They were hiking north also. Sharon, Kathy and I were the first to reach Cold Springs Lean-to, which accommodated only four people. We spread out our sleeping bags to make it obvious that we planned to spend the night. Shortly afterward, a young man about six feet tall and weighing two hundred pounds, approached and walked across our sleeping bags in his hiking boots. Putting down his pack, he said gruffly, "My group is staying here tonight."

With hands on my hips and fire in my eyes, I faced him. "We were here first, and the six of us are sleeping in this lean-to. There isn't room for more." I felt like a she-bear protecting her cubs. I didn't budge, and the silence grew more tense. "Stay where you are," I told the girls. The young man neither moved nor spoke again. When the rest of his group arrived, one of the members said, "Come on, we can go down the trail and find a place to camp." To our immense relief, he picked up his pack and left. Of all the people we have shared lean-tos and camps with on the A.T., he was the first truly rude person we'd met. Other hikers came and put up tents. We shared the lean-to with them, so they could cook and eat where it was dry, and the evening turned out to be comfortable for everyone.

The April sun woke us and we left early. Going through the little town of Wesser, we crossed the Nantahala River and started up the mountain. Morris Branch ran alongside the trail. Not knowing where the next water supply was, I suggested we look for a place to camp. Diane said, "There's a place over on the other side of the creek."

Mary asked, "How do we get there?"

"We'll have to bushwhack and cross the creek on stones," Kathy responded, "Let's go for it; it might be fun."

We found a perfect spot for our tents. The view down the mountain and the gently blowing breeze made us glad we were there.

According to the guidebook, we were about to start the roughest part of the whole A.T., a very steep, rough trail that would require considerable exertion. As soon as the eastern sky grew pink, we ate, packed and bushwhacked back to the Trail. We climbed a very steep section called the "jump up," which I had to crawl up. On the peak, the Trail followed a narrow ridge called Knife's Edge. I caught up when the girls stopped to rest on the ridge and asked, "How did you make it up the mountain so fast?"

Mary said, "It wasn't easy, but when we reached the top the feeling was unbelievable."

"It's peaceful and gives me a chance to think and talk to God," Laura added. "Climbing mountains is hard work, but you have to tough it out until you reach the top. There's no turning back."

"You sure can get rid of your insecurities," said Kathy.

"I enjoy hiking in the mountains," continued Sharon. "It gives you a chance to get close to nature and talk with your friends. Hiking mountains makes you reach down for extra determination."

As the day went on, the blooming flowers and spring air softened our struggle. The bare trees made vistas more plentiful. I couldn't begin to name all the wildflowers that had sprung up on the forest floor, but the Little Dutchman surely had a lot of breeches on the line. Passing Sassafras Gap Lean-to in the early afternoon, we continued along the rough trail to Locust Cove Gap. "Can we camp here?" Diane asked.

"Look for the spring before we decide," I said, "It's supposed to be a short distance down the mountain."

Kathy and Diane found water, and Mary, Sharon, Laurie and I put up the tents. We sat enjoying our wilderness campsite. In deep woods, miles from civilization, we were content.

We watched the big, red sun drop behind bare trees. "Do you think there are any bears around?" asked Kathy, crawling into the tent. "We're not far from the Smoky Mountains."

"There might be," I answered, "but the bears here wouldn't be like the bears in the Smokies. People haven't fed them, and they haven't had garbage cans to eat out of. Bears in the wilderness usually don't bother people unless they or their young are threatened."

"Good!" said Laura.

"And they really don't like strange smells," I added.

"You mean they don't like our odor?" Mary said, laughing. "It's only been four days since we've had a bath." We settled in and chatted back and forth. "Have you ever tasted an alcoholic drink?" Kathy asked Diane.

"Once on an airplane, the flight attendant let me taste champagne," Diane said.

"Did you like it?" she asked.

"I didn't have enough to tell," Diane answered.

"We serve wine at communion in our church," Mary said.

"Do they ever serve champagne for communion?" Diane asked.

Everyone laughed, and Diane was a little embarrassed, until I came to her rescue, "Papa and I both grew up in homes where alcoholic drinks weren't served, and we don't have them in our home either, so Diane has never had a chance to know."

"And we use grape juice for communion at our church," Diane added, having recovered her aplomb.

"We really didn't mean to laugh at you," said Mary. "I don't think it is necessary to know all about alcohol."

We left our cozy campsite early and continued our steep ascends and descends through the wildflowers that blanketed the ground. Upon reaching Yellow Creek Gap we decided to spend our last night at Cable Gap Lean-to, where we renewed our acquaintance with Bert and Jill Gilbert, an end-to-end couple we'd met at Carter Gap on a previous trip. End-to-enders hike the entire trail in one year. Bert and Hill were now rehiking favorite sections.

At first light, as our proud and happy band made a quick exit to finish the five miles to Fontana Dam, we reminisced about our accomplishments. We had held our ground with "the big guy," and had proved twice that we could camp alone, away from civilization. Last but not least, we learned that the roughest twenty-five miles of the A.T. were really not all that bad, especially in April when the wildflowers were in bloom.

CHAPTER EIGHT

Patty N., Kathy and Janet were the nucleus of a group who decided to hike north from I-70 in Maryland to Churchtown, Pennsylvania, a distance of seventy-five miles, across Center Point Knob.

Papa, driving John's car with four girls, and I, driving the station wagon with four girls, left on August 11 for the foot bridge where the A.T. crosses I-70 in Maryland. Around six o'clock P.M., the girls finished putting the food and tents in their packs and started hiking to the first lean-to. Papa, Lita, and I left to take the station wagon to Churchtown, Pennsylvania. By eleven o'clock P.M. we were back. Papa noted, "I've put you on the trail in rain, cold wind, and at all times of the day, but this is the first time I've left you in the middle of the night."

Lita and I stumbled along the dark trail by flashlight to Pine Knob Shelter where the girls were staying. With Lita in the group, we were bound to travel fast. Lita had graduated from college and wanted to hike on the A.T. once again before she started her career. Her hiking pace was as fast as when she was in high school.

On our first day on the Trail, we found the terrain was different—no grassy balds, but plenty of rocks to bruise our feet. A few hours after eating lunch on a projecting rock, we admired the splendid view of Middletown Valley, then Murphy's Law struck. Drue got a stomachache, Patty fell on the rocks and broke her glasses, Dawn had walked so fast she had blisters, and Jeannie A. was just plain tired. We found a little creek and made camp. Janet and Kathy found a pool of water under some branches, and with their biodegradable soap, took an Indian Princess bath.

The chirping of the birds woke us up, but we moved slowly. Everyone was tired and sore after the previous day's eleven-mile hike. Picking up speed as the morning progressed, we hiked on gravel road, then ascended steeply. From rock outcroppings and under power lines, we had snapshot glimpses of mountains. The Trail turned on to a road at Pen-Mar County Park and immediately crossed the Pennsylvania-Maryland state line.

In the afternoon Jeannie hiked slower and slower. It was five o'clock when Jeannie and I arrived at Bailey Springs where we planned to camp. The rest of the group was already there and wanted to change our plans and continue walking. Although Jeannie was limp with exhaustion, the consensus was to go on. Shortly afterwards, we noticed a black cloud and heard thunder. A storm was brewing. Jeannie and I were far behind. She staggered around, not moving more than a foot with each stride. Her face pale, her eyes half-closed, she lay down and gasped, "I'm going to lie here and die."

The wind from the impending storm cooled her. I gave her some crackers and wiped her face, saying, "We can't stay here; it's going to rain."

She mumbled, "I don't care. I can't move any farther. You go on and let me die."

At that moment there was a sharp clap of thunder. I quivered, "Jeannie, I can't leave you here. Try to walk. The rest of the girls can't be far away. I'll hurry and send someone back to help you."

I helped her up and she started walking as the clouds spewed forth a wall of water. Dawn and Janet, coming back to meet us, yelled through the thunderous rain, "Where's Jeannie?"

I called back, "Right behind me. Go help her."

The rain was torrential. The girls had two tents up; Lita and Patty helped me with mine. Before we had finished pitching my tent, we turned and saw Jeannie struggling up the slope, supported by the arms of Dawn and Janet, who now had Jeannie's pack on her back. I yelled above the pounding rain, "Take Jeannie's poncho off and get her in the tent."

Lita and Patty finished pitching my tent while I got Jeannie's sleeping bag and spread it out in the tent. As I removed her wet shirt and shoes, she was quivering and pale. I gave her a drink and some peanuts, M & Ms, and raisins; she ate a few bites and stretched out. While Dawn got in the tent with Jeannie and me, the other girls got in their tents, and we settled down to wait out the storm.

66

When the rain subsided, I checked the spring and found it muddy and unusable. We ate Spam on party rye and banana bread that Jeannie's mother had baked for us; this was our lunch menu for the next day. We had to eat in our tents, since it was still raining hard and another storm was threatening. Thunder rumbled and rain relentlessly pounded our tents. Drue appeared in the door of my tent. As she hurried to get in, she explained, "Our tent is flooded. There's a hole in the floor, and the water's coming in like a hole in a boat."

Making room for her, I asked, "What about the other girls in your tent?"

"They got in with Kathy, Patty and Lita," she answered.

There were now five people in one tent and four in the other. It was impossible to stay dry, but at least we were warm, crammed that close together. A loud clap of thunder popped right above our heads, then echoed endlessly through the mountains. Before it stopped, lightning flashed, and another clap of thunder pierced our ears. We were in a valley with a big tree over us. The wind bent the tree over, brushing branches against our tent. We lay there quivering. After another flash, I could see water running down the dirt road as the wind blew the tent flap open. The water leaped and jumped as it hit the rocks and splashed over the bank. Very little was said, but I could feel the girls quiver with each flash and boom. They kept their heads down in their sleeping bags, unaware that the water rushing down the road was about to overflow. I prayed that lightning wouldn't strike the tree. I expected to hear screams from the other tent but hadn't heard a sound. How could I, with the constant crash of thunder and pounding of the rain? I wondered how long this chaos would last. First, there was a flash, then thunder and constant creaking of tree branches; I hoped this wasn't going to be the end of our adventure. One bolt of lightning striking the tree or one big limb breaking off would mean disaster. "Oh! Don't let me think of such things. Please hurry and quit." Then a comforting thought came to me, This too shall pass. Soon the flashes diminished, the thunder subsided, and the rain slackened. Still, no one said a word. Everyone was completely exhausted. Whether they were asleep or not, all was quiet. It was much too crowded in the tent to move.

We welcomed daylight and a crystal clear day. This time when I checked the spring, it was clean. For our breakfast grace we sang, "God has created a new day, silver, green, and gold. Live that the sunset shall find us worthy of His gifts to hold." We enjoyed hot oatmeal and hiked to the next lean-to by noon. Lita, who had planned to return home at Caledonia Park, tried to persuade us to hurry to the park before night. Jeannie was still tired, and the others were also in need of a short day. On the third day I used my better judgment and previous experiences with personality problems and insisted we stay at Tumbling Run Lean-to. Drue, still having a stomach problem, decided to return home with Lita. Taking some food and a tent, they left to catch a bus back home.

The remaining group of seven cooked the dinner we hadn't eaten the night before, put up the tents to dry, and relaxed. We bathed and washed our hair in the creek. Patty, in her underclothes, was washing her hair when a man and his son came along. The man said, "I hope you're using biodegradable soap."

Patty shrieked, "Yes," as she looked for some clothes.

"I sure hope so," the man replied.

Seeing Patty's predicament, Jeannie grabbed a t-shirt and ran toward Patty, but the man and his son were already gone. The girls sat on the rocks in the creek, laughing and talking, with their feet splashing in the water. They were a happy group after living through the storm without panic, their self-confidence reaffirmed. Relief elicited from me another grateful "thank you!"

Later in the afternoon, we had a session on reading maps and the guidebook. The guidebook has some chapters reading from north to south and other chapters reversed. Jeannie and Patty planned where we could stay each day for the rest of the trip. Once the girls realized that the maps had contour profiles showing altitudes, they determined not only how many miles we had to hike, but also how many feet in altitude.

"I've hiked twice on the A.T.," Janet said. "and I want to hike as much as I can before I graduate."

"Yesterday afternoon I thought I'd die if I took another step," Jeannie added, "but today has been so relaxing, and after reading more about the trail, I think I'd like to hike as much as I can, too."

"I just like hiking," Kathy added. "It relieves a lot of tension, and we have lots of fun, even when it rains."

Learning, relaxing, and good fellowship filled the afternoon. After eating another hot meal, we retired on the floor of the lean-to with plenty of room for a good night's sleep.

It was an easy hike to Caledonia State Park. We stopped for soft drinks and candy bars, then we hiked on to Quarry Gap Lean-to. A light rain arrived about the same time we did, just enough to get the wood wet. Other hikers coming up from the park had trouble getting a fire started. Kathy, who was a real whiz at starting fires, amazed them with her Girl Scout skill.

We reached the next lean-to by lunch time but kept hiking. Pennsylvania was proving to be easy hiking. Maybe it was because the Keystone Hiking Club kept the trail in good condition. We spent the afternoon in the misty rain, eating lots of juicy blueberries along the trail. We had hiked over thirteen miles when we reached the two shelters at Tom Runs. Some boys already occupied one shelter, so we stayed in the other. It was built for four, but seven of us squeezed in to avoid putting up a tent in the rain. Shortly after dark, a noise awakened us. When Jeannie turned on a flashlight, the bright eyes of a raccoon peered at us. We watched him for a while then scared him away before he could get into our packs that we'd left outside.

The girls decided not to have a group Scouts Own. Each individual, while walking alone, would take the time to think some special thoughts. Giving the girls a chance to find their own personal space, I walked ahead and saw grazing deer and lots of blackberries. When the girls caught up, they were frantic. Kathy had gotten stung by a bee. The girls were afraid, she would have an allergic reaction. They had given her first aid, and by the time they got to me, Kathy seemed fine. I asked Kathy, "Have you ever been stung by a bee before?"

She answered, "No, and it really hurt and scared me. I don't know if I'm allergic to them or not."

Tagg Run Lean-to had two buildings, so we used one, but this time, we put up a rain fly. The creek in front was a perfect place for bathing and playing before supper.

We ascended a steep trail, traveled over a rocky mountain top, and reached Whiskey Spring, a large spring by the road. The girls wondered if it would be safe to camp so close to the road, but I saw no reason for concern.

This last night on the trail, we slept under the stars. While getting in our sleeping bags, we heard a strange noise in the tree right above our heads. There was a loud outburst, "Mama Boots, what was that?" I shined my light around but saw nothing. It must have been an owl that flew away.

Early in the morning, we passed the sign that said 1,000 MILES TO MT. KATAHDIN and 1,000 MILES TO SPRINGER MOUNTAIN, the midpoint of the trail. We climbed over protruding rocks on top of the mountain called Center Point Knob. Scrambling and hopping from one rock to another, we came to a steep descend on shale rock.

The remainder of our hike to Churchtown and to the station wagon would be on a road across the Cumberland Valley. On reaching the road, we saw a well-kept dairy farm with green fields, tall green corn, and white, neatly painted buildings. Jeannie bragged, "I'm sure glad I didn't quit with Drue and Lita. I really feel great about finishing the hike."

Dawn remarked to Jeannie, "You sure startled me the night of the thunderstorm. I was afraid you'd had a heart attack."

Patty said, "I'll always remember how much fun we had that afternoon at Tumbling Run Shelter."

Dawn laughed, "You mean when you got caught washing your hair?"

Felicity filled the air. Hiking in two states, across the midpoint and over seventy-five miles of the trail, was successful. Jeannie said, "Where can we plan to hike next?"

Kathy asked, "Why don't we hike over Springer Mountain in Georgia? Isn't that where the trail starts?"

"Yes, we did that section two years ago in December. Would you like to start plans to hike there after Christmas?" I asked.

Jeannie and Kathy responded quickly. "Sounds like fun. Let's go for it!"

*　*　*　*　*

On December 26, Papa took seven of us to Amicalola Falls. Kathy and Jeannie were in the group. The weather was very cold. Trees were covered with frost that dropped when the wind blew and formed ice on the ground, making hiking much harder. The sun shining on the frost made every tree look like a decorated Christmas tree, a breathtaking sight the girls had never seen. At night in our tents, we could hear the wind whistling through the trees with a fearful gale. As we started down Blood Mountain, the trail was covered with ice. Jeannie slipped and screamed. Kathy thought Jeannie was a goner, but Jeannie grabbed a tree and managed not to slide off the mountain.

As we packed the car for home, Jeannie asked, "When can we go to Maine and do the Northern terminus of the trail?"

"We have a group making plans to hike in Virginia during spring break. Maybe you'd like to start plans for a real adventure, going to Maine and hiking the Northern terminus in July."

Jeannie and Kathy answered in unison, "All right! Can we do it next summer?"

"It's a long drive," I replied. "We should plan a longer hiking distance. It'll take a lot of work planning transportation and food—and a lot more money."

The air buzzed between Kathy and Jeannie as they discussed plans for a trip to Maine.

CHAPTER NINE

Jane Tharp's troop was planning our April backpack trip in Virginia. Her girls called her "Thumper" because she wore her long hair in high pigtails when hiking. Thumper was an enthusiastic leader, anxious to get her girls involved in anything that was a challenge. Thumper drove her car, pulling a utility trailer filled with packs, with her daughter Jessica, and Debbie and Barbara from her troop. I drove my station wagon with Gail, Debbie D., and Michelle, from Troop 116, and five other girls. The girls started up the mountain where the trail leaves Virginia Secondary Road 652, while Thumper and I took the station wagon north to the James River where our trek would end.

The inexperienced girls soon discovered how different hiking at two thousand feet was in comparison to eight hundred feet in Jefferson County Forest. They found themselves breathless and their legs were refusing to respond to the hike command. Barbara B. kept saying, "This is stupid. I can't make my legs move."

Evelyn worried, "What's wrong with me? I can't get my breath."

Debbie groaned, "I wish I could go back home."

Jeannie A., who had experienced these same feelings several times, told them, "When you get used to the altitude change, climbing isn't bad."

By the time Thumper and I climbed Fullhardt Knob and reached the lean-to, the girls had recovered from the initial shock of the high altitude. Jeannie realized there was no water at the lean-to and went back down the mountain to get water for breakfast. I was very proud of her physical development and leadership skills.

Our first full day was short, so the girls' muscles had an opportunity to adjust to the changes from sitting in the classroom to hiking mountains. Sun and a cool breeze made ideal hiking. The Trail crossed the Blue Ridge Parkway at the overlooks, giving us unlimited views of the Virginia Mountains. Early in the afternoon, we came to Wilson Creek Lean-to in time for the girls to have fun in the cold water of the creek. We shared the lean-to with two men who had hiked in Maine. "What is the trail like in Maine?" asked Jeannie.

"There are a lot of muddy bogs, black flies that think they're mosquitoes and humongous mosquitoes," they told us.

Our canteens were crunchy with ice when we packed for our day's trek. Someone said the temperature was twenty degrees. Jeannie and Patty, the only veterans, led the trekkers. Shortly after eleven, I came to the group stopped for lunch. "Where's Jeannie and Patty?" I asked.

"They've gone on," replied Jessica.

An hour later we came upon Patty and Jeannie. Jeannie growled, "Patty and I've been waiting for an hour. We're starving!"

Jessica replied, "We stopped at eleven."

Jeannie snapped, "You were supposed to catch up to the leaders before you stopped."

Jessica retorted, "Well, I thought we were supposed to stop and eat at eleven."

"No, Jessica, the leaders stop at eleven," I interrupted, "When everyone catches up we eat lunch. I'm sorry, Jeannie. I thought you and Patty had eaten and gone on."

Patty and Jeannie were understandably upset to find we had eaten lunch without them. We gave them some food, but they were still quite angry. It dawned on me that this was the third day, as I tried again to explain the eleven o'clock ruling. It isn't only for lunch, but to check on each other and to be sure no one is lost or having any health problems.

During the afternoon we again became separated along the trail. Bobbets Gap Lean-to is located 1/4 of a mile off the trail. The sign to the lean-to was obscured by a limb. Everyone was there except Donna. I had maintained a position as the last hiker in the group, so I knew she couldn't be behind me. Her sister Beth said, "Donna was in front of me. She must have missed the sign."

Beth took off to catch her but returned alone. Jeannie and I then started searching in different directions. As Jeannie got to the road, a park ranger came by and stopped. She explained our problem, and he took her down the road where the trail crossed. There sat Donna, waiting for the rest of us to catch up. The ranger brought the girls back. Thanks to him and our prayers, we were all together. Bucket and Beth kidded Donna, who was a shy person, about having a secret rendezvous with the park ranger.

Bucket said, "It's mighty strange he knew exactly where Donna was."

Donna's face turned red. Everyone laughed and the tension over the day's mishaps was forgotten. But we made a new rule: The first person to find the sign to the lean-to would tie her bandanna to a limb or to the sign as a signal, and the last person would bring the bandanna to the lean-to.

In the early sun, we hiked more ridges. It was too early in the season for many flowers, and the buds on the trees were small, but the smell of spring filled the air, and the valleys showed signs of warmer weather. We stumbled down a rock outcropping with a view of Bearwallow Creek Ravine. Reaching the gap, the Trail meandered through mature trees and along Cove Creek.

I was writing in my log at Cove Creek Lean-to when Patty called, "Mama Boots, I forgot the macaroni for the stew. What can I do?"

I questioned, "Does the other group have macaroni? Maybe we can put both meals together and make the macaroni go farther."

Jessica responded, "We only have enough for us, and I don't want to be hungry."

Patty pleaded, "But without macaroni, we won't have stew. It'll be just soup and freeze-dried meat."

I interrupted, "Patty, fix the soup and meat, and we can crumble the crackers left from lunch to fill in."

We sang a Scottish grace, "Some have meat and cannot eat, some have none that want it. But we have meat and we can eat, and so the Lord we thanketh." The girls without macaroni substituted the word "macaroni" for "meat" in the grace. Patty's group crumbled crackers in the soup and declared it a learning experience on how to improvise.

On April 16th, with the sun beaming down through the trees, the temperature had risen to at least ninety degrees by noon. Under bare trees, we had no shade and the breeze was nil. Every mountain was a struggle. Our skin was clammy with sweat as we hunted for large trees and sat in the shade of the trunks. Gasping for breath, we felt something was wrong with us. Patty remarked, "I know I'm in better condition than this. There must be something wrong with me. I don't feel sick, but I can't get my breath."

"Our system can't take the sudden change from twenty degrees to ninety degrees," I told her, "Your breathing and that 'smothering feeling' will ease after you adjust to the change in temperature."

We made it through the day to Cornelius Creek Lean-to, hot, tired, and bedraggled. A meal and a cool evening relieved us. Jeannie was reading the guidebook when Donna requested, "Read out loud, so we'll all know what to expect."

Jeannie read, "Ascend steadily on trail. At 3/10 of a mile, cleared route of farmer telephone wire comes in on right. Ascend steadily. . ."

"Will you stop reading about those 'ass-cends.' I'm tired of 'ass-cending,'" Jessica interjected.

Everyone laughed and Barbara giggled, "We do seem to ascend more than we descend."

"Maybe that's because it takes twice as long to ascend as it does to descend," I commented.

We awoke with the sunrise, almost wishing it would rain. We began climbing the highest point of the Trail in this section. While we ate lunch on Apple Orchard Mountain, an end-to-ender named Steve, with his dog, Walker, stopped to take some pictures of the view from the overlook. I asked, "When do you plan to finish the trail?"

He replied, "About the middle of July."

I told him, "My group going to Maine hopes to be on top of Katahdin on July 27."

As Steve left we said, "Hope to see you on Katahdin."

We continued on in the heat, following a ridge for miles. I hoped everyone had plenty of water to prevent dehydration and heat exhaustion. Late in the afternoon, we came to a very steep mountain, eliciting groans and sighs. Michelle let out with "Oh my gosh! Do we have to climb that?"

Barbara added, "My blisters hurt and now another disgusting mountain."

The rest of the girls, several with blisters, also complained, and I even heard "heckie durn." I wondered if we would make it up the mountain, but the girls reached down for the extra strength to make the summit of High Rock Knob, then down to Marble Spring Lean-to. The spring had cool water to wet our parched throats and to use for cooking food, but not enough for splashing. The disappointed girls piled up some leaves and unrolled their sleeping bags for a night under the stars. I could hear the girls chatting. Debbie said, "I can't wait until I get home to tell my friends what I did on spring vacation. They won't believe me, but I'm proud of my accomplishment."

"I wonder if we'll see Steve again when we get to Maine," Jeannie said to Gail.

"I doubt it," said Gail. "That's more than three months from now."

Morning was still hot and dry, and the forest was like a tinder box. We came to a creek near the bottom of the mountain and Jessica pleaded, "Can we jump in?"

The station wagon wasn't far away, and most of us were anxious to get home, so we didn't take time to splash. As we walked the last few miles, we recalled the events of the trip. The girls had learned the importance of being concerned for each other, how to be forgiving and stay friends. We had hiked fifty-one miles in temperatures ranging from twenty to ninety degrees, and we had climbed 4,000 feet. I wondered how many of this group would be going to Maine.

$$* \quad * \quad * \quad * \quad *$$

After months of planning and recycling aluminum cans and newspapers, painting a garage, and washing cars to make money for transportation, we mailed food supplies to a fishing camp and left for Maine. Thumper had such a good time in April she decided to go to Maine with us and helped with all the planning. We spent several mornings laughing and talking about the trip as we crushed aluminum cans. Thumper and I each drove a station wagon, meeting at a rest stop on I-71, outside of Louisville, to begin our three days of travel.

Driving along, I thought about the girls in the group. Diane was home from Morehead University for the summer. Bucket, Donna, Jeannie and Gail had been on the April hike. Kathy was back after hiking over Springer Mountain in December. Carmel H. was on her first hike. We stopped at Salisbury, Massachusetts and camped at an overcrowded campground on the beach.

Jeannie and Carmel wanted lobster for dinner, so we found a restaurant where everyone picked out the lobster she wanted, a first-time adventure for most of the girls. Fascinated and eager to try the delicacy, they restlessly waited and read the restaurant's bib explaining how to eat lobster. When their lobsters came, they used the nut cracker to crack the claws and the little fork to dig out the meat in the legs. Breaking open the tail, they worked their way around the hard shell, retrieving the sweet meat without missing a single bite. Kathy, who had eaten lobster before, whizzed right through, helping some of the others who were having trouble. Carmel asked, "Do you eat the meat in the tail?" as she

75

dug down with a questionable expression, wondering if there was anything there to eat.

Diane, holding up what appeared to be just a shell, asked Kathy, "How do you get to the meat in here?"

All the "ahs" and "ohs" and expressions of delight drew the attention of a man who, at the end of the meal, walked over and said to the group, "I've had a delightful evening watching you learn how to eat lobster. You did a good job."

Pointing to Kathy, he said, "You've eaten lobster before; you knew what to do. Your a good teacher."

The girls laughed as their faces turned red, and Kathy said, "I didn't know anyone was watching us."

Kathy wrote in the log:

> Exiting the interstate, we had our first glimpse of the tip of Katahdin. Farther on, we could see how big, steep, and beautiful it really was. Our stomachs churned and our lungs breathed heavily as we got closer. When we reached Baxter State Park, we took our food and extra clothing to Katahdin Stream Campground, so we wouldn't have full packs hiking over the mountain. Next, we went to Roaring Brook Campground where we would stay the night. Diane, Bucket, Thumper, and Jeannie took Mama Boots car to Monson where we would end our hike.

When they returned from Monson, Jeannie and Bucket filled the air with stories of seeing moose, dodging big lumber trucks on a narrow gravel road, and of barely making it back before the gate to the park closed.

In my sleeping bag, I prayed it wouldn't be raining in the morning. If the weather is bad, the park service closes the trails on the mountain. We were going to be terribly disappointed if we had to use our alternate plan.

It was daylight at four-thirty A.M.. I looked at the sky and decided it wasn't going to rain any time soon. After waking the girls, we started to Chimney Pond, where we would find out if the weather would permit hiking on the mountain. The Cathedral and Saddle Trails were open, and we chose Saddle Trail, the longest but supposedly the easiest.

Looking straight up at the big boulders, Gail asked, "Is this the trail?"

"There's an orange flag up there between the rocks," Kathy answered.

"Watch the loose gravel," Diane screamed over the howling wind, "if you slip, you'll be back down the mountain."

Inch by inch we made it up to the timberline. Kathy and Diane came back and warned, "Be careful! The wind will bowl you down!"

Not only was it windy, but the mountain was enshrouded with clouds that blew past us with cutting speed. Kathy found a big boulder to shield us, and we searched our packs for our heavy jackets and gloves. Like drunks we slipped and stumbled on rocks and were knocked over by fifty miles per hour winds as we followed the little orange flags. When we reached the trail to be used in inclement weather, Jeannie yelled above the wind, "Are we going to use the cutoff trail? The weather is really bad."

"As long as I can stand up and still see the little orange flags, I'm going to the top," I replied. "I've traveled this far, and I'm not going to miss seeing that sign on the northern terminus of the trail."

When we reached the sign, there sat Steve, the hiker we had met in Virginia. Jeannie and Bucket yelled out, "Steve, you made it!" and everyone joined in to congratulate him.

I asked "How does it feel to have finished the A.T.?"

"I'm glad to finish because all my clothes are worn out, and I'm tired of backpack food," he responded. Then his expression changed and he said softly, "I'll miss being on the trail. It gets to be part of your life. Something you don't want to part with."

Looking through breaks in the clouds, I imagined a spectacular view if the day had been clear. Steve agreed and we recalled the number of mountains we'd been on in the clouds.

Kathy and Jeannie began following the white blazes of the A.T. across the flat tableland above the timberline. Some of the girls were out of sight when we reached the edge where the Trail starts down Hunts Spur. We couldn't believe it! White blazes were going from one big boulder to another out into space. A strong gust of wind parted the cloud, and we got a glimpse of Kathy, Carmel and Diane climbing around, under and between gigantic building-size boulders. For two hours we climbed, slid, crawled and prayed, at times hanging on for dear life to iron hand holds drilled into the rocks. At one particularly steep boulder, I pointed to the rock below and suggested to Jeannie and Thumper, "Let's take off our packs. I'll slide down first, and you hand me the packs."

Except for the scary glimpses when wind separated them, the clouds kept us from seeing how high we were, and how straight down it was on both sides of the spur. Thumper promised, "Lord, if I ever get off this blasted mountain alive, I will never, ever do this again."

Jeannie quivered but didn't say much when she saw Kathy and Carmel jumping from one rock to another as though it was great fun. Gail's short legs wouldn't reach from one rock to the next, so she had to slide, and the seat of her pants was wearing thin. Donna ripped the seams of her pants while stretching from one rock to another. Battered and frazzled, we reached Katahdin Stream Campground totally exhausted.

We planned a day of rest. Jeannie started the day with a few exercises to loosen up the muscles before getting out of the lean-to. Kathy built a fire to dry our clothes. Diane got out the needle and thread to mend everyone's pants, while Jeannie, in charge of planning our menus, divided the food we would be carrying. Gail and Bucket put up the tents to dry, and Thumper and Donna were in charge of watching the clothes hanging by the fire, while Kathy and I gathered wood. Everyone packed for our trek of over 110 miles. The weather cleared in the afternoon, and we again got a good look at Katahdin and Hunts Spur. We couldn't believe what we'd done.

After a good night's rest, we got an early start. We had 12-8/10 miles to hike. The terrain was basically flat but muddy. We stopped at an inviting stream to take a bath and wash our hair in the cold, but refreshing, water. Kathy, who was more daring than most, didn't consider that we were beside a road. She had only her panties on when a car stopped, so she made a mad dash under the bridge and nearly froze while the people in the car sat there talking.

We stopped at Abol Bridge Store to send postcards home, get some additional oatmeal, and savor our last soft drinks before starting into the Northern Woods of Maine, the beginning of the longest wilderness section of the A.T.. We forded several streams, occasionally slipping on the rocks and falling in, but the bogs really grabbed our attention. To follow the trail through the bogs, you look across the big mud hole and find a blaze indicating the direction of the trail. You hug the trees and hop from roots to rocks, or give up and walk straight through the deep mud.

At daylight, we left Hurd Brook Lean-to in a misting rain. Ascending to the top of Rainbow Ledges, we could see five lakes or ponds in the mountains and all the way back to Katahdin. Blueberries were plentiful and Diane gathered some in a plastic bag for breakfast the next morning. Most of the day was spent walking around Rainbow Lake in the bogs.

The sound of the rain on the tin roof lulled us into a restful sleep. At daybreak we hiked on, eating wild red raspberries, hiking in bogs, rain, and mud most of the day. When we got to Nahmakanta Lake Lean-to, a family was there on vacation, so we put up our tents overlooking the lake. The "no-see-ems," little tiny bugs that bite like the devil, and mosquitoes big as jet planes drove us into our tents. Insect repellent didn't faze these bugs. The back of Jeannie's legs looked as if she had measles. I could hear the girls laughing in their tents, having a tickle fight and a fun time in spite of bugs and bogs.

It was hard to get out of the tents when morning came. Kathy, Jeannie, and Carmel, our speed hikers, were last to leave camp. The Trail was on a gravel road that turned to dirt, then back to the bogs. As the group hiked along, Jeannie said, "I'm not going to get my boots wet today. They almost dried last night. If I try real hard, I bet I can make it through the day without getting in mud over my boot tops."

We came to Tumbledown Dicks Brook, and Bucket said, "Here's your chance to get across without getting your feet wet."

Jeannie stopped, sized up the situation and jumped to the first rock. Landing high and dry she bragged, "So far so good. Now if I can just make the next one." Splash!! "Well, maybe tomorrow I can keep my shoes dry."

Jeannie wasn't the only one to give up keeping the boots dry. When the Trail came to a muddy swamp, Kathy said, "I'm not even going to try. I'm just going to walk straight through the mud." Her foot slipped and "kerplunk" she was on her knees crawling out of the mud.

Bucket bragged, "I can do better than that!" as she landed on her behind. We were all in danger of following suit as we struggled to contain our mirth watching her attempts to get to her feet in the slippery mud.

"Take your pack off and hand it to me, then maybe you can get up on your feet," I managed to giggle. Kathy and Jeannie pulled and Bucket finally emerged from the mud.

It was lunch time when we reached Potaywadjo Spring Lean-to in a steady rain and declared the rest of the day a day of rest. Carmel, who had a good voice and knew many songs, started singing. After lunch we sang ourselves to sleep. Later in the afternoon, we discussed religion. We had several different denominations in the group, and after comparing our religious customs, Diane said, "I don't see a whole lot of difference. We all believe in the same principles, very much the same as the Girl Scout Laws."

Jeannie asked, "Is it proper to pray for it to quit raining?"

We came to the conclusion that if it strengthened our faith, why not? We were sure to get either a yes or no answer. During supper, several backpackers came along who were wet to the bone. Jeannie asked, "Would you like to eat under the shelter," but they chose to eat in their tents.

Two boys, John and Craig, surprised me by asking, "Are you Mama Boots?" They had read the log book at Katahdin, and when they caught up with a group of girls, they figured it must have been "Mama Boots and Company, Kentuckiana Girl Scouts," since that was the way I signed the log book.

Monday morning the sun was shining. Our prayers were answered, but the mud was still with us. At Cooper Brook Falls Lean-to we took a bath, washed our hair, and tried to swim, but the water was too swift. John and Craig came along about supper time and put up tents. Some of the girls talked to them about how far they were hiking, and where they were from. Jeannie and Carmel were busy carving off knots and smoothing the handle of a walking stick.

Jeannie gleamed as she greeted Thumper in the morning, "Happy Birthday, Thumper. Kathy and I made you a new walking stick. It's stronger and doesn't have knots like the old one."

Thumper laughed, "I wondered what you and Kathy were doing in the tent last night. I really appreciate this because my knee still hurts."

Thumper had been suffering from "A.T. knee" since Hunt's Spur. During the day, we met several end-to-enders. I always asked, "When did you start the trail, and when do you expect to finish?"

Most answered, "I started in April and hope to finish by the middle of August."

Now I also asked, "Do you know Steve? He was hiking alone, a medium-sized, blond young man."

Greg, from New York, asked, "You mean Steve Wisell from Massachusetts?"

"I don't know his last name, but we met him in Virginia last April and told him we would be on Katahdin the 27th of July. When we got to the summit, there sat Steve."

Greg laughed, "Now we know why he slowed down. He could have finished at least a week earlier. He must have wanted to meet a group of girls."

John, an end-to-ender from Georgia, said, "I kept reading about Steve but couldn't catch him. I gained on him in New Hampshire. That must have been when he slowed down."

End-to-enders keep track of each other by leaving messages in the log books. Sometimes they never meet the person, but they read entries each night and get to know each other through the log.

John and Craig caught up and ate lunch with us; they were delighted by our homemade strawberry preserves. We reached East Branch Pond Lean-to and considered hiking farther but voted to stay. We sang "Happy Birthday" to Thumper and had spaghetti, Thumper's favorite dish, and tapioca pudding. Everyone quieted down and Diane said, "Someone's putting up a tent. Let's go see who it is."

It was Paul and Gary from Cincinnati. Kathy built up the fire for the boys to cook on and had an interesting time discussing the different careers they were going to pursue.

Morning found us nervous about fording another river. Thumper suggested, "My walking stick seems to make it easier to keep my balance on the rocky bottom of the streams."

We all picked up a stick along the shore and managed to get across East Branch without falling. We were getting used to walking in water up to our knees. This was the day to pick up our food supplies. When Diane and Kathy arrived at White Cap Mountain Lean-to, they emptied their packs, and the rest of us stashed our packs inside the shelter. With the two empty packs, we hiked to West Branch Pond fishing camp. Returning to the lean-to, Gail and Donna divided our new supplies, and we were soon packed for another six days of hiking. The next day we would climb our first mountain since Katahdin.

Jeannie, Kathy and Carmel reached the blue-blazed trail to the summit of White Top Mountain and hiked up to the fire tower to see the view. Diane, Donna, and I followed. From the fire tower we could see lakes, ponds and marshland. Jeannie pointed to the north and said, "I bet that's Katahdin over there. The only high mountain around."

Kathy, looking southwest, remarked, "I bet we'll be climbing those mountains next."

Carmel said, "It's a relief to climb mountains and get out of the bogs."

We returned to the trail and caught Thumper, Gail, and Bucket, who had hiked on slowly. After lunch, we hiked straight up and straight down over Hay Mountain, West Peak and Gulf Hages. The New England trail doesn't have long switchbacks like in the south, but the altitude is only about 3,000 feet. We made camp by a stream. While Kathy, our chef for the night, was preparing the meal, the rest of us sat on the rocks in the creek. Watching the flowing water, we recalled the events thus far and anticipated what would follow.

Everyone's eyes were swollen in the morning, probably caused by the weeds growing in the creek. I lit the backpack stove for a quick breakfast, and we started hiking in the rain. Soon the swelling left our eyes. After fording West Branch Pleasant River, we reached Pleasant River Road. Thumper's knee was still bothering her, and she was going to get off the trail, but the gravel road looked like it wasn't traveled very much. Jeannie said, "You can't get off here. You could be here for a month before anyone would pick you up."

Thumper agreed. Picking up her birthday walking stick, she said, "I can make it with the help of my stick."

Hiking through more bogs on our way to Chairback Lean-to, Kathy saw a moose in Long Pond, but she slipped and it ran away before the rest of us could see it. High enough in altitude to see a sunset, we sat on a big rock behind the shelter and watched the sun disappear behind the mountain.

After a very restful night, we started climbing the rocky steep terrain of the mountains. Eating lunch in the cold mountain air, we hurried to Cloud Pond Lean-to. Kathy, Diane, Donna, Bucket, and Carmel spread out sleeping bags while Diane, Kathy and I pitched a tent for the rest of the group. Two guys came in and said, "We're end-to-enders. You have to get out of the shelter and give it to us. Camp groups are not supposed to use the shelters."

"We're not a camp group. We're a group of hikers," I answered.

"The shelters are put here for end-to-enders," one guy snapped, "Other hikers are supposed to carry tents."

I retorted, "I've been a member of the Appalachian Trail Conference for almost ten years, and I've never read anything about end-to-enders having special privileges."

"We don't have a tent to protect us from the rain," he said.

"You've got to be kidding," I laughed, "There's no way you could hike all summer without carrying a tent or tarp to protect you from the weather."

They had no answer, but wrote some unkind remarks in the log book about a group of Girl Scouts who would not give them the lean-to. They finally left and put up their tarp beside the pond.

We spent the evening singing for Skip, his father Bob and co-worker Gary. They were from Dover-Foxcraft, Maine and worked for the paper company in Millinocket. They had gotten to the lean-to before us but pitched their tents so we could have the lean-to. Bob said, "If those guys hadn't left, Gary and I were ready to step in and assist you, but you handled them very well."

The next-to-last day of our hike, we got a fast start. After ascending and descending, we passed Bob, Gary, and Skip eating lunch, and continued down a gravel road, relieved we weren't hiking in the bogs. Bob, Gary, and Skip then passed us while we were eating and gave us some insect repellent made for the insects of Maine—mosquitoes, "no-see-ems," and black flies. We camped the last night at Little Wilson campsite.

I didn't have to awaken the girls. They were anxious to get to Monson. We expected an easy day, but the bogs were worse than any we had been through. There were no logs or rocks. We had to walk straight through and hope for the best. Gail, sinking into the mud to her knees, yelled, "Mama Boots, I'm stuck."

Not wanting to get stuck myself, I suggested, "Pull hard and see if you can make it out."

She pulled, and with a loud sucking sound, her foot came out. Fortunately her boots stayed on. It was raining so hard we could hardly see each other, and we were beginning to wonder if we'd make it through our last day. Finally, the bogs ended and the trail followed an old stage road which, after all the rain, ran with water like a creek. Seeing the black top road leading to Monson was like seeing a long lost friend, the first hard surface road in ninety miles. The nine of us packed into the station wagon and headed back to Baxter State Park. I dropped the girls off at McDonald's in Millinocket, where they learned about Bella, a hurricane that had hit the coast and caused all the rain we had walked through.

Thumper and I went to get her car and had a good laugh as we recalled gathering aluminum cans and newspapers, driving three days and walking in the rain and mud for two weeks. When we returned to McDonald's, Diane had found a motel that would take nine dirty, muddy people for the night. As we drove to the motel, Gail said, "I thought I was a goner when I got stuck in that mud. I thought Mama Boots was just going to let me stay, but her encouragement helped me get myself out."

"Sometimes I thought I wasn't going to make it," Donna added, "but meeting those end-to-enders who had hiked all summer gave me determination to go on."

"I think I'm hooked," Carmel said. "I can't wait to tell my sisters about Maine."

We had loved Virginia in April, but our Maine experience was definitely the most challenging trek so far. The trip had been a real adventure, fourteen days in the most remote part of the Appalachian Trail.

CHAPTER TEN

In April, at the junction of Virginia Highway 42 and secondary road 631, we discovered the trail had been moved. I'd read in the *Trailway News* that there was considerable rerouting in Southern Virginia. Using my forest service map, we found the Trail several miles farther up the road. The girls started up a forest service road to the Nidey Lean-to while Thumper and I took the van north to Virginia 652 where we'd finish hiking.

Thumper and I talked about the girls as we climbed to the lean-to. Jessica and Debbie B. were hiking again. Lisa G., Diane G. and Michelle B. were new hikers from Thumper's Troop. Michelle, Debbie D., Gail, Vickie, Sheila and Shrimp, were from Troop 116.

Jeannie A., now a senior in high school, greeted us at the lean-to, "The map on the wall shows the latest rerouting of the trail. It's different from both the guidebook and the forest service map."

Thumper, Jeannie and I tried to determine the shortest way to the A.T.. Jeannie measured the distance on the map with a string and estimated about ten miles to the next shelter if we went east on the blue-blazed trail. We hiked two and a half hours before we reached the white-blazed A.T.. Michelle said, "I'm hungry!"

Thinking it was only five miles to the next lean-to, we enjoyed a leisurely lunch beside a small creek. Crossing a road, we saw a sign indicating it was eight miles to the next shelter. At Craig Creek, I called the group together and discussed our situation. "We have a problem. The trail has been changed since the guidebook was published," I said, "We can camp here and know we have water, or we can hike eight miles to the next shelter. If we camp here, we'll have to add another day to our trek."

Jessica remarked, "The creek is large enough for some real fun. Let's stay here."

Shrimp added, "I don't want to hike eight more miles."

Lisa G. asked, "Would there be water between here and the shelter? Maybe we could hike a couple of miles farther."

"I have no way of knowing, since we have no map or guidebook that shows the new trail," I answered.

"It's the first day of the trip. Why kill ourselves until we have to?" Michelle added, and the group started playing in the creek.

We moved along on freshly graded trail in the morning. Arriving at the lean-to early in the afternoon, the girls raced to play in the creek. Thumper, Jeannie, and I started comparing the map, signs, and guidebook and discovered that a considerable amount of new trail had been added over Cove Mountain. Jessica said, "Why can't we stay here? I don't want to hike any more."

I explained, "If we don't hike farther we will have a twenty mile day in order to finish by Saturday."

Vickie asked, "Where will we stop for the night? Is there another lean-to?"

"I don't know. The only information we have is on the sign, and no lean-to is mentioned," I answered, "I just hope we can find water and a place to camp."

We set out on a long climb up another mountain with a Buzzards Rock on top. By the time we reached the top, Shrimp was about to pass out. She said, "Can we stop. I don't think I can make it. I'm hot and thirsty."

"I'm tired," Sheila added. Thumper fixed lemonade, and we sat and rested. Michelle asked, "Can I go on ahead and see if I can find some water?"

"That's a good idea," I said, "Time yourself and come back in thirty minutes. I don't think this group can hike much longer."

Michelle returned without finding water. I could hear their tired, disgusted groans and moans as we trudged along the ridge. By six P.M., the girls were nearing total exhaustion. I found a place on top of the mountain where we could pitch our tents and advised the girls, "We can stay and camp here without water, then find water in the morning, or we can keep on hiking."

"Let's stay here. I can't move another inch," Shrimp sighed.

"This situation is worse than Maine," complained Gail. "We had too much water there, but I'd rather have too much than none at all."

Jeannie suggested, "Let's eat our Spam on party rye and snacks to save our water for drinking, rather than cooking noodles for stew."

The unhappy group crawled into their sleeping bags. A cool breeze made it easier to get up the next day. Michelle, who was writing the log, described the morning:

> We started without water, walked without water, and finally crawled without water, but when the first of us made it to the bottom of the mountain, a real nice lady gave us a drink. Did it ever taste good!
>
> The lady was helping us refill our canteens when one of us pulled out a canteen that was still full. We were outraged that she'd had all that water and didn't share it when we were all so thirsty. Vickie reminded us that Mama Boots and Sheila still didn't have water. Taking a canteen, she and I headed back up the trail to meet Mama Boots and Sheila.

Up on the mountain Sheila had decided she was going to lie down and die. She said, "You go on; I can't take another step."

I gave her the rest of my water and said, "Come on, we're going down, and we'll soon be at the bottom of the mountain where there's a road. I'm sure we'll find water."

The trail turned, and we saw a big rock protrusion called the "Dragon's Tooth" and Michelle and Vickie coming up the trail with some water. When we came to a little store, everyone drank and ate for about an hour.

Sheila said, "I can't go any farther. I want to go home."

Jessica added, "I'm tired of hiking."

Jeannie said, "The girls voted and want to quit."

Feeling that they needed this experience to learn how to cope, Thumper said, "That's too bad! Mama Boots and I are going to keep hiking. We're not going to hitch a ride to get the car."

I tried to encourage the group, "We'll only hike a short distance and make camp before we start back into the mountains."

By a slim majority, the girls agreed to continue hiking. Some walked very slowly, grumbling all the way. Sheila lagged behind, barely creeping, even though it was easy walking. Within two hours, we came to a creek and set up camp in a pasture. Vickie, Lisa and Jeannie went back to a farm house for water. With all the dried cow pies around it was hard to find a place to pitch our tents. After supper we splashed in the creek, and I heard the girls laughing. Vickie asked Jessica, "Did you really hide your freeze-dried peas under that cow pie?"

"Yes," Jessica giggled, "and Michelle B. put her stuffing under another one. After all that food at the store I just couldn't eat that backpack stuff."

According to the map, we had twenty-one miles to the van. The guidebook said twenty-three miles. If the guidebook was right, we'd have a thirteen-mile hike the following day.

We broke camp early and immediately began a steady ascend up Catawba Mountain. My watch stopped, making the time one more thing I didn't know. Reaching the road, the group stopped at a small restaurant and had sandwiches and salads, raising their spirits a smidgen.

I read in the guidebook, while eating my salad, about a restaurant and realized the book and the trail were back together. It would be a thirteen-mile day. Sheila continued to hike very slowly. We needed to do something to speed her up or it would be dark before we reached the lean-to. I gave her my flashlight and told her, "Walk as fast as you can, but if it gets dark, sit down by a tree and turn on the flashlight. I'll come back to help you after I put my pack down. I can't walk this slow."

It was a rocky, steep climb up McAfee Knob, but Sheila kept up. At the top, I pointed to a distant cliff and said, "I bet before the day is over we'll be on that cliff."

We passed through a fissure in the rock outcropping and came to a fire road. Much to our relief, two forest rangers, "angels of mercy," came by in their truck and gave us water.

All afternoon we climbed over, around and between cliffs and outcroppings. The many overhangs gave us the feeling of walking through space. We traipsed cliff ledges bearing names such as "Snack Bar Rock," "Devil's Kitchen," and "Rock Haven." By the time we reached the protruding cliff I had pointed out earlier, the sky was turning pink, a gentle breeze was stirring, and the mountains and green valley were peaceful. Sheila had kept up all afternoon.

"I've hated every minute of this hike," Sheila said, "but I've never seen such vivid views of the mountains. It's hard to explain, but I'm glad we didn't quit."

I smiled and said, "You may never go backpacking again, but you'll always remember how beautiful Virginia is from the top of Tinker Mountain, and the feeling you had when you reached the top."

We reached the lean-to around seven-twenty by Thumper's watch, and everyone had a good laugh. I'd said all day we would get to the shelter by seven-twenty, the time my watch had when it stopped.

Michelle wrote in the log:

> When we got to the lean-to, it was getting dark, and the whole state of Virginia must have known by our screams that we'd finally reached water. For dinner we had Jeannie's specialty and Thumper's favorite—spaghetti. Mama Boots even remembered to bring the Parmesan cheese. What a feast! For dessert we had chocolate and butterscotch pudding. Then all fourteen of us crammed into the lean-to and slept.

An early morning whippoorwill woke us, and we hiked along Tinker Ridge with unobstructed panoramas of the valley coming alive with Spring. The girls were ahead of Thumper and me when someone screamed, "Mama Boots!" We rushed in the direction of the scream, expecting to find someone hurt, but Michelle was expressing her joy at the endless view of the long valley below. "I feel like an athlete," Michelle said, "I've always wondered how it would feel to play in a big sports event and win. Now I know how ballplayers must feel when they win—physically challenged and successful."

"See that brown field over there?" Michelle added, "I bet the farmer has just plowed it. There's another field that's real green."

"Look at the different colors on the mountains," Shrimp said. "At the bottoms they're green. Then there's a reddish look, and on top the trees are bare and gray."

"That's caused by the different temperatures on the mountains," I explained.

We devoured lunch on another outcropping, viewing a lake with boats that looked like ducks. A week of searching for water, and here was this large lake! It was a very ironic ending to a thirsty week. I hoped a new guidebook would be available soon. I hadn't realized how much we depended on the book until we didn't have one.

*　*　*　*　*

91

Final plans were complete, and in July we departed for Dover-Foxcraft, Maine, the home of Bob Nelson, a friend we'd met on the Trail in Maine two years ago. Thumper drove her van, and I drove the faithful station wagon. After three days on the road, we arrived at Bob and Lois's, where we set up camp in their front yard. It was our last experience with civilization until we would get to Gorham, New Hampshire, 180 miles south. The girls would spend the next day in Monson, while Thumper and I dispatched vehicles. Jeannie asked, "Can I go with you? I'm Thumper's co-leader now that I've graduated from high school."

"It's all right with me," said Thumper.

I said to Harriet, a dependable person with good leadership skills, "You and Suzanne take the group up the trail this afternoon and make camp. It may be late before we get back."

We parked the van at Grafton Notch and could see the sheer wall of Speck Mountain. "Oh, my gosh!" Thumper said. "Do we have to climb that wall?"

"I hope not," replied Jeannie. "It looks really hazardous."

"I doubt it," I said, "the Trail usually goes around such steep places."

"I'm afraid of heights," said Jeannie. "Remember how much trouble I had on Hunts Spur coming off Katahdin two years ago?"

Bob picked us up at Maine 27 where we parked the station wagon and brought us back to Monson. We picked up some extra insect repellent for warding off Maine insects, put on our packs and hiked to the girls' campsite.

Heading south through Blanchard on an old lumber road, Torri, our first time hiker asked, "What made those big animal tracks?"

Harriet, on her first New England hike, questioned, "Could they be moose tracks?"

Donna, who had hiked in Maine before, said, "That's what it is. We might not see a moose, but I'm sure we'll see their droppings."

We were looking for a spot to make camp when it started raining. Everyone put on her poncho and sat down to wait out the storm. The rain stopped and Carmel yelled, "I've found the creek. It has plenty of water."

As the girls pitched the tents, Nancy asked, "Where's the other tent pole?"

It was a frantic and useless search. We'd need to improvise. Jeannie called, "I think I've found a stick that'll work. It's a little short, but it'll hold the tent up."

The climb up Maxie Bald Mountain over granite ledges in the early sun surged circulation and deepened breathing. Descending to Joes Hole Lean-to, we found it occupied and hiked on to Maxie Pond. The ponds in Maine are great places for a nice evening swim. The boys at the lean-to came down to swim also, adding to the evening.

The day's trek started at sunrise on a gravel road, then an old tote road, across Little Sandy Creek and up Pleasant Pond Mountain. We moved right along to Pleasant Pond Lean-to and decided to hike on to Caratunk to pick up our first food package. Peggy G. and I stopped to cool our hot, tired feet in a creek. She said, "I can't wait to see the mountaintops in New England."

"I hope I can get into this trip," I confessed, "I feel worn out from all our troop activities this summer. I didn't have time to participate in the planning, and being in on the planning is what gets me psyched up."

"You'll feel better when we start climbing the mountains. I know you," Peggy answered, "backpacking is in your blood."

When Peggy and I arrived in Caratunk, Thumper and Jeannie had gotten the food box and found a place for us to camp on the banks of the Kennebec River. The river was too dangerous to wade, so we arranged with Mr. Smith to meet us at eight A.M. to take us across by boat. On the other side of the river, we strolled along and reached Pierce Pond Lean-to by lunch. We were going to have an afternoon for laundry, bathing, writing in the log, and rest.

Jeannie read about Mahoosuc Notch in the guidebook. She was worried and told the other girls, "When Thumper, Mama Boots and I were at Grafton Notch, we saw this gigantic steep cliff on the side of the mountain. I'm afraid the trail might go over it, and I don't know that I want to do that. The book says it's dangerous and requires substantial physical exertion."

Peggy said, "By the time we get to the Notch we'll be in good physical condition. Why worry now?"

The discussion started some unrest. Torri said, "I don't know if I'll do that or not."

Leading us out at sunrise, Donna suddenly stopped and said, "There's a bear!" Sure enough, there was a bear with its paws on a tree eating bugs. When the bear heard us it ran off into the woods. At a private camp, I asked, "Is there a good place nearby where we could camp?"

The proprietor replied, "Follow the Portage Trail for about a quarter mile after the A.T. turns off, and you'll come to the shore of East Carry Pond. That's a good place."

After breakfast, Harriet, Nancy, Torri, and Suzanne, group one, wanted to retrace the Portage Trail to the point where the A.T. turned off. They didn't want to take any shortcuts. Group two had hiked the trail to the gravel road the previous afternoon and followed the road. Group two missed the turn off. "Has anyone seen a blaze recently?" I called.

Thumper answered, "No."

It's a mistake that happens quite often on the A.T.. You're following a nice gravel road and forget to watch for the blazes. This time we were split, and a mad chase was on to get everyone together. Group one didn't know they were in front. I told Carmel, "You're a fast hiker; hurry and try to catch them."

Carmel ran to catch group one who were running to catch group two. Carmel caught them by lunch time. We laughed as we ate, and Carmel told us about yelling for Harriet's group. Harriet added, "When I heard Carmel's voice behind me, I wondered what was going on. We were hiking as fast as we could to catch up when all of a sudden you all were behind. I knew we hadn't passed you."

We climbed through a boulder–filled ravine to the top of Little Bigelow Mountain. The view of the Carrabassett Valley, Flagstaff Lake and several nearby mountains rekindled my excitement at being on the A.T.. Peggy was right; I felt I was where God wanted me to be—on a wilderness adventure with girls. Harriet and Carmel led us down the long descent between the mountains. We were almost to Flagstaff Lake before the trail turned and started up Avery Peak. It took us three hours to hike the 1-8/10 miles to the Myron H. Avery Memorial Lean-to.

We sped out of the col, a pass between two mountains, toward West Peak, with the mountains engulfed in clouds. We felt our way from blaze to blaze. The blazes were painted on rocks up and down several peaks called horns. Some ate blueberries, while others searched for the blazes and then called to the berry eaters. This procedure continued while crossing the Bigelow Range. Thank God for the volunteers from the Maine Chapter of the Appalachian Mountain Hiking Club who had painted the blazes.

We came to the station wagon and packed a nine-day supply of food, then started the next leg of our trek. The packs were the heaviest any of us had ever carried. When we put our feet down we felt we'd go right through the mountain from all the weight on our backs. Torri said, "I can't believe I'm carrying this."

"If this food was really good it might not be so bad," Shrimp added.

"Be thankful it's as light as it is," Nancy remarked, "If we had to carry canned food, it'd be worse."

Peggy sighed, "The other side of the earth must be having an earthquake from the weight of our packs."

The Trail down Crocker Cirque was on rocks that would scoot out from under our feet. The bottom of the cirque was at least a hundred feet straight down. We held on to each other and occasionally sat down and used our hands to keep from going to the bottom head over heels. We shared the campsite with Ray from New York who had a harmonica. Carmel led the group singing, and Ray played along until the rain drove us into our tents.

Fording the Carrabassett River, we started the long ascend up Sugarloaf Mountain. Carmel and Harriet, the first of our group to arrive at Spaudling Lean-to, came back to meet us. Harriet said, "We don't want to stay in the lean-to. There are a couple of crazy guys there."

Carmel added, "They're dressed strangely—old business suits and rubber boots, instead of the usual jeans and hiking boots of backpackers."

We squeezed all four tents in a spot only big enough for two and hoped it wouldn't rain. We were glad when morning came. The girls thought the men might be on drugs. We talked about drugs and their effects on people. The girls were quite knowledgeable on the subject, but this was our first encounter with someone using them on the Trail, and it was disconcerting.

Harriet turned the conversation to a more positive tone, "I'm addicted to the feeling of confidence I get hiking, and I know how to feed that—just keep hiking. I get high enough just being on top of a mountain, and that's a high that won't let you down."

Coming to Orbeton Stream, we bathed and ate lunch before starting the climb up Poplar Ridge. When we reached Poplar Ridge Lean-to, we had hiked for eleven days and had eleven more planned.

We hiked above the timberline on Saddleback Jr., the Horn, and Saddleback. The guidebook said the open summits were magnificent, but the only thing we could see were the white blazes. The lack of visibility was no longer fearful; instead, we acquired an angelic feeling about walking among the clouds that left little drops of water on our eyelashes and hair. The cairns, stacks of rocks with white-painted blazes on them, were like the hand of God leading us across the mountain. We called back and forth to each other and listened to Peggy, the comedienne of the group, telling us about the antics of her cat, Ralph, and what he would do in a situation like this. She even talked as if she were the cat, a fun diversion from the stresses of climbing and feeling our way across the open summits.

Near Piazza Rock Lean-to, some caves had been formed by rocks which had fallen from the cliffs above. Shrimp, Peggy, and Torri checked them out while Jeannie and Suzanne talked to Greg and Andy, who were hiking in the same direction, about the dangerous Mahoosuc Notch. Nancy, Donna and Carmel were helping Harriet write the log. Harriet, who had been reading the guidebook, said, "I can't believe it. Since we added our food supply, we've hiked seven peaks 'with a net elevation gain of over 10,000 feet.' Doesn't that sound great. Just look what we've done."

Nancy added, "I knew we were doing a lot of climbing. But it went fast when we were above the timberline in the clouds."

It rained all night and morning found us very wet. Gloom set in again. I'd read that end-to-enders have times when they become depressed and want to quit because of rain and bad days. This was that kind of day for me. Harriet, reading my mood, said, "Let's start hiking. It'll quit raining and everything will be better."

"Let's not stop for lunch in this rain," I told the group, "Eat your snacks, and when we all get to the shelter we'll have lunch."

The group had split into speed hikers and slow hikers. Thumper walked with the slow hikers, and the fast hikers were in front of me. The slow hikers were carrying the lunch. They stopped and ate lunch, thinking the speed hikers were deliberately trying to make them hike faster.

When I reached Sabbathday Lean-to, Harriet, Carmel, Donna, and Peggy were there. Nancy was right behind me. Harriet asked, "Who has the lunch? Can we eat when everyone gets here? I'm hungry."

An hour later the slower hikers came in. "Where's lunch," Peggy asked.

Torri answered, "We ate it. We were hungry, and you all didn't stop."

"Didn't you hear Mama Boots say not to stop in the rain for lunch? She said we'd have lunch when we all got to the shelter," Harriet responded.

"No," answered Jeannie.

Pulling out the remainder of lunch, Shrimp said, "Here's your share of lunch."

Carmel remarked, "Jeannie, you were one of the fastest hikers when we were hiking two years ago. You and Kathy were always the last to leave in the morning and the first to arrive at the shelter in the afternoon."

Jeannie didn't answer, and I wondered if our problem was caused by too many chiefs—with the other girls caught in the middle. We should have had a "Scout's Own" to discuss the problem and stress the importance of being considerate of each other, but we were busy drying out tents and clothes.

Thumper informed me she was worried about her grandmother and was getting off the trail the next day to call home. I should have discussed the problem with her, but I kept telling myself that everything would be okay in the morning. I hoped Thumper would change her mind and stay with us and that the problem between the girls would disappear. When we reached Maine Highway 17, Thumper got off the trail with Greg and Andy. She remarked, "If I can find a telephone close, I'll call home and come back to the trail, but if not, I'll get the station wagon and meet you at Grafton Notch."

I felt really down. Thumper getting off the Trail left me with the total responsibility for the group. We took our time going over the four peaks of the Bemis Range. The trail was rocky and the sun was bright. I was on a mountain range, not in the clouds, but my emotions were cloudy.

All the girls except Jeannie and Suzanne were at Elephant Mountain Lean-to. We had been there for almost an hour, and I was getting worried. "There's no need for them to be that far behind," I thought.

This time there was a genuine problem. Suzanne had broken her glasses, and Jeannie had led her all the way to the lean-to. Jeannie spent the evening putting the glasses together with rawhide. Now Suzanne had a pair of goggles.

We descended into the valley and crossed Maine Highway 5. The Trail went through a swampy area and passed a beaver dam, a relief from being in the clouds. Jeannie and Suzanne remained at the brook after lunch for a long time. At Squirrel Rock Lean-to I took a nap while Shrimp, Carmel, and Peggy entertained themselves, climbing on the big rock behind the lean-to.

We resumed our trek early, hiking on a worn lumber road through pine trees. At Frye Brook Lean-to we found a natural water chute and several waterfalls in the gorge behind the shelter. The girls had a good afternoon playing in the water and lying in the sun. I did some mending on my pack, but my biggest worry was Suzanne's glasses. So far the rawhide was working, but she needed the glasses to walk.

Trying to keep the group together, I told the girls in front to stay close and the ones behind to speed up. We had a lot to do when we got to the van. First we passed the Churn, a narrow cascade dropping through the chasm into a deep pool, then the Cataract over ledges in the brook. Next came the Flume, a spectacular sheer falls in a narrow canyon. The other falls were not named, but we marveled at the many falls on Frye Brook. We left the small brook and fired up to climb the twin peaks of Baldpate Mountain. Iron ladders were placed on the ledges to climb up the side. Once on top above the timberline, we could see back to the Bemis Mountains and ahead to Old Speck and the Mahoosuc Range.

When Peggy and I caught up with the other girls, Torri, one of the slow girls, had given Jeannie her part of lunch and left the rest of the group behind. "You girls need to cooperate with each other," I scolded, "Jeannie, why didn't you encourage Torri to stay with the group? We never let one hiker wander off alone."

Jeannie shrugged and said nothing. "We need to talk about this and figure out how to work better together," I added, but no one was in a talking mood.

After lunch we had a rocky steep descent to Grafton Notch. Thumper was waiting with bad news. The van had been broken into and some of our food had been stolen. One of the men at Spaudling Mountain Lean-to was hiking in the same direction as we were and had asked how we planned to get more food. We made the mistake of telling him where our food supply was. "Next time we don't tell anyone where our vehicles and food are located," said Harriet.

We changed into the clean clothes which were in the van, packed the food that was left, and got organized before Jeannie and Thumper took the station wagon to the end of the trek. Everyone had gained the courage to go through Mahoosuc Notch in spite of the perceived danger. Thumper and Jeannie found a store and returned with peanut butter, jelly, and crackers to replace our stolen food.

We had jam cake and fresh milk for breakfast which gave us a good start for the last twenty-five miles of our trek. Thumper stayed behind and said she would meet us at the parking lot on New Hampshire Route #2 where the trail crossed the road.

We started the steep 2,000 foot climb up Old Speck Mountain. The prominent cliff we had seen when we parked the van was visible, but we didn't climb it. The "eyebrow" has a sheer 800 foot drop to the floor of the notch. We reached the North Ridge and climbed steadily toward the summit. Jeannie, Torri, Suzanne and Shrimp took the 3/10 mile trail to an open observation tower with a spectacular view of the wild area of New Hampshire and Maine, while the remainder of the group continued on.

Peggy remarked, "We're finally going down. How much farther to the lean-to?"

I replied, "I hope it's close. I'm getting tired of climbing over these shrub-covered boulders."

The front group reached Speck Pond Lean-to around three o'clock. The next day we'd be hiking the Mahoosuc Notch, a deep cleft between Mahoosuc Arm and Fulling Mill Mountains. Giant boulders from the notch's sheer walls clogged the floor of the notch, which necessitated a climb over and under these obstructions. Ice was in the caves formed by the rocks. This was considered the roughest mile of the Trail. We were beyond the point of no return, and our excitement mounted.

We left in a hurry and ascended Mahoosuc Arm Mountain, then had a steep descent into the notch. Harriet laughed, "Mama Boots, you look like a toddler climbing steps, crawling up one big rock and scooting down the other side."

I watched with envy as Carmel, with the balance and grace of a ballet dancer, hopped from one big boulder to another. In places we had to remove our packs, push them through the caves that had been formed by the rocks, then crawl through. After all the worry about this part of the trail being dangerous, the girls were having a great time. Harriet's description:

> The notch was like a big rock playground. You had to go over, under, around and between big boulders. It was great!

It was a steep 2,000 foot climb up Fulling Mill Mountain before we'd reach Full Goose Lean-to. The front group arrived around three o'clock. Several people were already there, so we didn't save spots for the slow group. A man at the lean-to told us the trail had been rerouted and several miles were added. The group at the lean-to figured how we could still finish the trail as planned, but it would be necessary to hike more than five miles a day. The slow group came in about five o'clock and had to pitch a tent.

At sunup, I told the slow group we were going to skip the next lean-to in order to finish on time. They would have to speed up. Jeannie expressed her anger. I took her aside and explained it was the girls decision. As adult leaders we had to accept their decision. I kept both groups in front of me all day. It was only nine miles and we had hiked over 150 miles. No one had any physical reason for being slow. We hiked across the Maine-New Hampshire border and over Mt. Success before we reached Gentain Pond Lean-to, a very modern shelter with a loft and a nice pond to bath in. Another new structure was a 2001 solar john. The latrine was constructed in a manner that would allow the sun to speed up the decomposition process. Everyone seemed to be happy that we had come on to this shelter. The girls sang and chatted as they fixed the evening meal. It was only two short days to the end of the trek.

The caretaker of the lean-to told us about a new campsite half the distance to Route #2, so we planned to camp there the next night. The trail to the new campsite was easy after the steep climb of the previous two days, but blueberries along the way made going slow as we stopped to eat the juicy ripe berries. It was a brand new campsite, and we had it all to ourselves. Jeannie and I rested in a tent while the girls played charades. I commented to Jeannie, "The girls seem to be having a good time together. Do you know what the problem was all about? You were with the slow group."

Jeannie replied, "Maybe the slow ones were afraid of the Mahoosuc Notch, or maybe they just didn't want to hike very far each day."

"I was wondering whether some of the girls might be having a hard time accepting you being a leader. You're pretty close to their age," I said. "Being a leader isn't easy. You have to follow the girls' suggestions and try not to just tell them what to do."

Jeannie was silent and I continued, "Sometimes you even have to step back and let them communicate with each other and solve their own problems without your help."

We silently listened to the girls laughing outside. I sighed and relaxed. "Whatever the problem, it seems to be okay now. They sure sound like they're having a good time."

On the fifth day of peanut butter and jelly for lunch, we were thankful for a nice patch of blueberries. On Hayes Mountain, we sat looking down at the little town of Gorham and over at Mt. Washington, the next big mountain on the A.T.. I wondered how soon we'd be back to tackle that mountain.

I arrived in Gorham a little after the others and found Carmel was crying. "What's wrong?" I asked.

She told me, "I dreamed last night that my grandfather died. I found a phone as soon as we got here and called home. My grandfather is okay, but my grandmother had a stroke and isn't doing very well."

"I'm sorry," I said. "Do you want to start home right now?"

"No, I want to go to church."

Suzanne asked around and found a church that had evening services. We ate at McDonald's, and went to the motel to clean up, then went to church with Carmel. I looked around at the girls and thought about the experiences, good and bad, that we'd shared. I reflected on the way the girls had matured in their ability to get along with each other and to appreciate the value of friendship. They had learned a lot about nature and themselves, as had I, and now we were here with Carmel when she needed us. I said a prayer of thanks for these girls and for their continued learning experiences.

CHAPTER ELEVEN

For five years during April spring breaks from school or when school closed for the summer in June, we hiked the Trail over the ridges in the State of Virginia. The Trail is not too strenuous, and the sights and smells of the coming season are refreshing and invigorating.

Jessica, Barbara from Thumper's troop, and Vickie and Carol from my troop, planned a fifty-eight mile trek from Pearisburg north to Craig Creek. We crossed New River and started a steep ascend. The first day and a half was an uphill climb. At the top of the mountain, we had a Scout's Own. The theme was love. Vickie remarked, "My mother gets really mad at me, but I still love her. Sometimes, I wonder if she loves me, the way she fusses, but I know she does."

Barbara added, "I wonder if my parents hate me because I don't clean my room or do the chores around the house."

"They may hate what you do or don't do," Thumper said, "but they still love you."

I added, "Sometimes I run out of patience and fuss at the girls in my troop because they don't clean the dishes the way I'd like them to, but I still love each one. Nothing can change that."

We added to our list, to love nature and the importance of doing our part to protect the balance of nature. "We need to be careful of our streams," I told them. "We shouldn't get soap from our dishes in the water. Good fresh water is going to get more scarce if we don't protect it."

Carol said, "Someday I think I'd like to be a forest ranger and learn more about how to protect the trees from disease and insects."

Barbara joined in, "It's so beautiful in the mountains. I can understand now why it's important to carry all your trash out of the forest with you."

"Yes, it would be a shame to leave stuff here that would spoil it," Jessica added.

We continued hiking along the crest of the mountain until we came to a blue-blazed trail where we found water and made our camp, high in the mountain. After dinner, the girls returned to the creek to clean up and get water for breakfast. Thumper and I cleaned the dishes in the big orange plastic bucket while listening to the girls laughing as they splashed in the creek. Thumper asked, "Have you hiked in Pennsylvania?"

"Only about fifty miles," I answered. "Have you?"

"Last summer while you and the Senior Scouts were in Europe. Michelle, Pam, Nancy and I started at Harpers Ferry, West Virginia and hiked to Duncannon, Pennsylvania, 120 miles," she said.

"Michelle's hiked with me several times. She's developed into a really dependable hiker and takes a lot of responsibility," I responded.

"She surely does," Thumper replied. "She planned our menus, and bought and repacked all our food for the trip. She did an excellent job."

"Do you think you'll ever be able to say you've hiked all of the A.T.?" Thumper asked.

I shrugged, "I'm in no hurry, but if I keep putting bits and pieces together—who knows. My main interest is to help the girls experience the excitement of hiking on the A.T.. They're so elated when they reach their hiking goal. It gives my ego a real boost to have helped them do it."

By morning it was raining as we hiked over Peter Mountain and descended to Stony Creek Valley on our way to Baily Gap Lean-to. We arrived cold and wet and immediately got into our sleeping bags to get warm before supper. After thirty minutes in the sleeping bags, Jessica, Barbara and Vickie braved going to the spring for water, while Thumper, Carol, and I fixed supper without getting out of our sleeping bags. By the time we retired for the night, it was sleeting. Using our flashlights, we lay in the lean-to and watched the sleet bouncing on the picnic table, hoping it would be warmer tomorrow.

The trees, decorated with frozen clouds and sparkling crystals of frost, glittered in the sun. The water jug was frozen, as well as our boots, jeans, and canteens. It was a challenge to fix breakfast with frozen water, but we were soon walking in the cool morning air. We found a lot of wild animal tracks, deer, wild turkey or grouse, and possibly wild boar and bear. We wished we could see some of the animals.

By noon the sun had melted the frost on the trees. As we ate lunch at the site of an old fire tower, Jessica sighed, "I wish I had a hamburger instead of this chicken spread."

Vickie said, "Not me, but I'd sure like a pizza."

Barbara added, "I miss 'Bonanza' and eating popcorn."

Carol and I decided we'd like an ice cream cone. After a long lunch break, we descended to War Branch Shelter for the night.

At first light, I started the stove and put on the water for instant oats and hot chocolate. I heard Vickie say, "Is that Mama Boots out there rattling those pans? It can't be morning already."

Carol yawned, "That's her and I see pink sky. I guess we'd better start rolling up our sleeping bags."

We climbed over rocks on top of the mountains, then descended and ascended by crawling on our hands and knees in the mud. Crossing a fence on a stile, we followed an old road that crossed the creek on an old covered bridge. At Highway 42 near Newport we camped in the recreation area. Thumper and the girls walked into the little town for some snacks while I cleaned the dishes. They returned with a big box of caramel popcorn for me.

In the morning, we climbed straight up to the crest of Sinking Creek Mountain. While walking along the rocky ledge and slanting rock, I looked up and said, "Oh my gosh! Where's the trail?" Big trees sprawled in every direction.

Vickie called out, "What's wrong? Do we have to climb through those trees?"

Pointing to a distant, uprooted tree, Jessica said, "There's a white blaze on that big tree. The trail must go in that direction."

Thumper questioned, "How do we get there?"

Barbara said, "I'm going to try to get above the brush at the top of the mountain and see if I can get through that way."

I replied, "It's pretty rocky up there. I think I'll try to go below."

Vickie and Carol followed me. I cautioned them, as we started below the brush, "Keep your eyes on that tree with the blaze, so we can find our way back to where the trail's supposed to be."

Thumper and Jessica started straight through the brush. Barbara called to Thumper, "The rocks are really big, slick and sharp this way."

Thumper responded, "I'm having a hard time finding a way through the brush, too."

The tree branches were thick and bushy, catching on our packs and clothes. Vickie, Carol, and I decided to work our way back to the trail by walking on the trunks of the large trees. Vickie yelled "Help!" and I looked around to see her hanging by her pack frame. She had slipped; the frame caught on a branch, and she was left dangling.

Carol called, "I'm right behind you. It may take me a minute, but I'll help as soon as I get through this jungle."

We struggled for hours to get through the maze of rocks, downed trees and brush. The drizzling rain made the tree trunks and rocks slick, and we kept stepping on our ponchos as we tried to step up on the downed trees. We could hardly find the white blazes to know if we were going in the right direction. Frustrated and tired, everyone wondered if this was the A.T. or a wilderness jungle. Suddenly, it turned into a neatly cleared trail. The Roanoke A.T. Trail Club had been busy clearing the trail after a winter wind storm. The ordeal was over and about an hour later, Jessica found us a place to camp.

The trail club hadn't had time to finish their job, and we came to more downed trees. It had rained during the night and everything was wet—jeans, ponchos, and shoes. We again slipped and slid on the slick tree trunks and rocks, catching our packs and clothes on limbs. Everything was tangled up, making us wonder if we'd ever get out.

We came to a scenic spot with green pines and blooming white trees. A small brook ran through this quiet spot. In the stillness I could almost hear a voice saying, "Keep hiking with scouts, and keep working to educate girls on the importance of preserving the wilderness for the future." Inwardly, I said "thanks" for whatever led me through that beautiful spot at just the right moment. My faith reaffirmed, we headed for the car more aware of how difficult it must be to keep up the trail.

*   *   *   *   *

One evening Jeannie A., who was now attending the University of Louisville, called and suggested, "Let's plan a trip somewhere on the A.T. for June. I want to get some more miles."

"Have you hiked across Rhododendron Gap?" I asked. "I have three girls interested in a hike. I was going to suggest that to them. The rhododendron are so elegant in June."

"I'd love to see them," said Jeannie.

"Come to our meeting, and we'll find out if the others would like to hike among the rhododendron," I said.

June came in a hurry, and we were soon on the way to Grindstone Campground where we picked up Dudley Caldwell, a Sierra Club friend, who took us to Elk Garden where we'd start hiking north. He would pick us up at Big Walker Lookout at the end of our trek.

We hiked to Deep Gap Lean-to for our first night, and at daylight we started climbing Mt. Rogers. The trail had been moved to protect the delicate forest floor of Virginia's highest mountain and no longer crossed the summit.

Soon we were at Rhododendron Gap—still my favorite part of the trail. As Jeannie and I walked across the gap, I asked, "Wouldn't this be a beautiful place for a wedding? The trail could be the aisle."

Jeannie, pointing to a nice green spot with a large rhododendron bush right behind it, said, "That would be a nice place for the ceremony. But if I got married up here, how would my guests find the place?"

I said, "I'd be the usher if I only had to make one trip."

She added, "We'd have to bring my mother in by helicopter. She wouldn't be able to hike up the mountain."

As we hiked the next day, we passed Comer Falls where I recalled the fun M.S.'s group of girls had cavorting in the water when I was here before. Sometimes I wondered why I kept repeating parts of the trail, but each time we had hiked this section, it's had special meanings.

We soon found ourselves at Raccoon Branch Lean-to, and during the night, we heard a honking noise I couldn't identify. Ray Miller, a fellow hiker, said, "It's a deer." We had seen lots of deer but this was the first time we had heard their call.

Chirping birds woke us and soon we were on new trail rerouted away from Teas. The first pleasant surprise was a sweet cherry tree filled with ripe cherries which made a great mid-morning snack. Carala, Regina and Peggy were ahead of Jeannie, Mr. Miller and me. When we caught up, Carala, a first-time hiker, said excitedly, "I saw a big snake. It crawled right across the trail in front of me. Scared the heck out of me!"

"I saw a deer looking me straight in the face," Regina said. "I stopped and stood still, but when I reached for my camera, the deer ran off. I've never seen one that close."

We spent the night camped near the ranger station, then hiked through dark-orange and lemon-yellow azaleas, white rhododendron, and pink and white mountain laurel. Though they were rookies, Carala and Regina climbed over Brushy Mountain, Locust Mountain and Glade Mountain with an air of confidence.

It was raining when we came to I-81, and we decided to spend the night in a motel. Staying in a motel in the middle of a trek was a first time experience. After a delightful restaurant meal, we returned to the motel and listened to the pouring rain as we drifted off to sleep.

Leaving the motel, we followed a road that went under I-81. The trail turned off the road to follow a small creek where a troop of Boy Scouts were packing up sleeping bags and tents soaked by the rain. We ascended Mt. Gillian and Walker Mountain, walking in the clouds with a breeze blowing mist across our faces, to Walker Mountain Lean-to. The Boy Scouts, arriving right behind us, had baffled looks on their faces. After we'd passed them, they decided they'd overtake us and get to the lean-to first. With all their efforts, they didn't make it. One of the boys asked, "How did you stay dry in all that rain last night?"

"We stayed in a motel," Jeannie told them.

"You cheated," another boy said. "You're not supposed to stay in motels when you're hiking the A.T.."

Jeannie laughed. "We believe in doing what's best to stay dry."

The leader comforted his boys. "That's probably the reason we couldn't catch the girls—they weren't carrying wet sleeping bags and they had a good night's rest."

The boys built a fire to dry out their sleeping bags, and we helped hold the bags around the fire. We exchanged samples of backpack food and chatted about hiking the A.T.. Some of the boys bedded down in the fire tower, others in the lean-to. It had quit raining, and everyone was dry.

After breakfast, we started along the ridge crest of Walker Mountain for our last day on the trail. Peggy and I walked together recalling other hikes we'd taken together. "I can remember you keeping the group in a good mood by telling witty stories," I recalled. "It seemed to keep their minds off the steep climbs, rough terrains and inclement weather."

Peggy said, "I remember constantly asking 'How much farther to the lean-to?' You always answered, 'It's probably just around the next bend.' Your patience and constant encouragement is awesome."

"What I liked most," Peggy continued, "was the feeling of being on top of the mountain. It proved to me that I could meet a challenging goal. What seems like an insurmountable goal can be reached by simply plowing through and refusing to give up."

"Why did you decide to go backpacking?" I asked.

"I saw it as an exciting new experience. I'd never hiked more than a day at a time. Backpacking sounded like a great adventure," she said, "and it really is."

We came around a bend in the trail, and there was Mr. Caldwell walking up the mountain to meet us.

*　　*　　*　　*　　*

The girls in my Senior Girl Scout Troop had one more year until they graduated from high school. When September came, I decided to take a Cadette troop, ages twelve to fourteen, and my Seniors finished their last year as a Senior Patrol. The new girls heard the Seniors talk about backpacking and decided they wanted to try it also.

Karen, the secretary of the group, wrote to the church in Pearisburg, Virginia and inquired about the hostel they furnished for hikers. Cathy Walker, a Girl Scout leader who belonged to the church, answered her letter and agreed to help with housing, shuttling of vehicles and anything else we might need. She also asked if Emily, a girl from her troop, could hike with us. The night before our hike we stayed at the hostel.

We hiked north from Big Walker Lookout on Virginia Route 21, planning to finish at Pearisburg. By three in the afternoon, we arrived at the lean-to. The Piedmont A.T. Trail Clubs had built a cistern, but for some reason there wasn't any water in it. I read in the guidebook about water down an old road. The entire group got canteens and the water bag and looked for the water. It was much easier to find than expected.

After breakfast, we walked in the mystical world of rain and clouds. When we reached High Rock Lean-to, it was still cloudy, and we again found no water in the cistern. Jeannie A. had hiked this area and had told me about the Ramseys who lived in the valley. They had let her camp by the creek near their home. We decided to see if we could camp there. We came down the mountain, and the clouds and fog turned to steady rain. I'd heard it was possible to walk in clouds above the rain, but this was the first time we had experienced it.

Sherri, a tall, thin girl with lots of spunk, slipped on a rock while crossing the creek and fell in. She got up laughing but her sleeping bag was wet. We were quite happy to come to the mailbox with "Ramsey" written on it. I asked

108

Mrs. Ramsey if she had a dry place for us to camp. Mrs. Ramsey said, "You can sleep in the garage."

She let Sherri dry her sleeping bag in her dryer and invited us to use her stove to cook our supper. Her hospitality was greatly appreciated.

Morning dawned clear and for two days we followed the familiar white blazes in sunshine. Rerouting along the trail made our hiking distances uncertain at times, but we arrived on schedule at Doc's Knob Lean-to late in the afternoon of the second day. At lunch on our last day, we discovered that a mouse, the most dangerous animal we'd encountered, had eaten the peanut butter right through the plastic squeeze tube while we slept.

Descending Pearis Mountain to Pearisburg, the girls charged ahead. Emily had promised to take them to Walker's Drugstore for ice cream floats. I followed the trail to the Sears sign. Carmel H., who was hiking in the area with her sister Theresa, had driven my car from Big Walker Mountain to Pearisburg. Emily's Girl Scout Troop brought a supper of sloppy joes, baked beans, potato chips, carrots and brownies to the hostel. After our feast, we played volleyball and got to know the girls in Emily's troop. It was a great way for my young girls in Troop 116 to end their first A.T. hike.

*　　*　　*　　*　　*

Seven of us were ready to travel to the Shenandoah National Park for another fifty-three miles. Jeannie A. was with us again. Two sisters, Sharon and Donna D., Laurie, Tammie, a girl from Troop 116, and Gayla, a Brownie leader and Day Camp Director, were first time backpackers.

When we got to the entrance of the park we saw a big sign—NO BACK-COUNTRY CAMPING. Tammie had sent for and received a camping permit, but the weather had been very dry since she'd received it. It had rained all night, but we found the ranger to get permission before we started our northbound hike. Most of the trail in the Shenandoah was originally cleared by the Potomac A.T. Club in late 1920. With the construction of Skyline Drive, sections subsequently had to be relocated, most of the work being done by the Civilian Conservation Corps (CCC). Much of the cribbing on the side of the trail was still in good condition despite the trail being used by thousands of people over the years. We pitched our tents at Sawmill Run Lean-to, probably the only people to share the park with the animals that night.

"Why did you decide to hike on the A.T.?" I asked Laurie.

"I was looking for a more challenging experience than the usual Girl Scouting events," she answered.

When we reached the top of Blackrock Mountain, Laurie commented, "Whew! What a difference! This is invigorating. I didn't know I had so much determination."

"I've never climbed a mountain before," Tammie said. "The muscles in my legs are getting tight. It's a lot different from walking at home."

"It's so peaceful here," Donna said. "Nobody to tell you to do this and do that."

For several days the girls viewed the valley through the bare trees and from the many overlooks along Skyline Drive. The spring rain kept the air fresh, and wildflowers were starting to peep through the earth. The last day of the trek, Tammie and Donna were leading the group up Baldface Mountain, the steepest mountain in this section. Their speedy pace mirrored their feelings of confidence and physical well-being. Reaching Lewis Mountain Campground, after hiking fifty-three miles in the Park, we realized we had been the only people hiking.

*   *   *   *   *

Vic Bayers, an end-to-ender I'd met in New England, joined us at U.S. Highway 522 near Front Royal, Virginia, where I'd parked my car. He took us to Lewis Mountain Campground where we would continue our trek north through the park. Gayla Baker was back again and Mayo Lynam, a Scout leader who had backpacked in the Grand Canyon, was along. We had three girls who were eager to experience the A.T. for the first time.

It was much colder, and all the little waterfalls were frozen. We shared one campsite with a snowman someone had built and left to greet us. Carol was a confident hiker and led the group most of the way, even though this was her first backpack trip. At Mary's Rock, the trail started a 1200 foot descent into Thorton Gap. "Good!" Marie exclaimed. "We're going down. It's easier."

"What goes down soon goes up," I said. "I'd rather stay on top of the ridges."

We spent our last night at Gravel Spring Lean-to. In front of the shelter, deer grazed in a large meadow. Carol gathered some grass and walked up to one, getting close enough for a good picture.

We got into our sleeping bags, laughing and talking about the events of the day. "I like backpacking," Wilma said. "It's a challenge. You have to plan ahead, yet take what comes each day. Perseverance can accomplish anything if you focus on it."

Wilma's shoes were coming apart, and next morning I took all the adhesive tape we had and taped her shoes, hoping they'd make it through the trek. It would be another thirteen mile day, but there were no major climbs. As Carol and I approached the park boundary, we saw something black climbing a big tree. It was a black bear. We watched it climb into a hole at the top of the tree. About four o'clock, we came to the car. Wilma's shoes had made it. "I knew they would," she said.

As we rode home, we recalled our new experiences: we'd learned that bears don't always sleep in caves but can climb trees and sleep up there. We had been close enough to deer to hand feed them, and the weather had been exceptionally good for this time of year—pleasant temperatures and no rain. Carol put it into words for us: "Hiking the Trail has made me believe I can dream big dreams and make them come true."

*　　*　　*　　*　　*

Carol wanted to continue hiking north, so she helped a group plan a trip from Route 522 near Front Royal, Virginia to I-70 in Maryland, a distance of seventy-five miles. Melissa was the only novice in this group. "Do you think you can hike that far in a week?" I asked her.

She grinned. "I don't know, but I'd like to try."

As we walked along, Carol pointed to an animal grazing in a field. "Is that a zebra over there, or am I seeing things?"

"It's a zebra," I said. "The chain link fence marks the boundary of the National Zoological Research and Conservation Center. We might see all kinds of different animals."

We reached the site where the shelter was supposed to be, but it had been destroyed by fire. We put up our tents in the rain and cooked under the rain fly in the door of one of the tents.

It was very wet at sunrise though the rain had stopped. The Potomac Appalachian Trail Club was in the process of rerouting this section of the Trail from the Shenandoah National Park to Harpers Ferry, so with no up-to-date, detailed information, all we had were white blazes. Hiking beside a stone fence, we came to a sign saying, DO NOT DISTURB STONE WALL. G. WASHINGTON WALKED HERE. Rocks had been evenly placed one on top of the other, making a perfect fit without any mortar. Even now, not one rock protruded or seemed loose.

We walked on Virginia Secondary Road 601 after a restful night near a gently moving stream. Even after leaving the road, the terrain was fairly level below the rocky ridge visible through the trees. We hiked among early spring flowers, and every so often a short trail led to the top of the ridge where we could get a view of the Shenandoah Valley. Moseying along in the warm April sun, we passed the place where we'd planned to camp. Around four o'clock we found a spring. Mayo, a biology teacher, looked at the spring and said, "I think we'd better keep going to Keys Gap Shelter. This water doesn't look usable."

We hiked seventeen miles, but the next morning we skipped 2-1/2 miles of the Trail and followed the blue-blazed trail into Harpers Ferry to visit the A.T. National Headquarters and tour the historical part of the little town. Jean Cashin, the receptionist at A.T. Headquarters, told us about a youth hostel on the other side of the bridge.

In the early morning, we walked the C & O Canal Towpath. Restored as an historical park, the Towpath had been built along the river in the early 1800's. Mules had pulled boats up river from Washington, D.C., to Harpers Ferry. Now, the Towpath was used as a hiking trail. We hiked it for three miles before starting up Weverton Cliffs, our first steep climb of the trip, with sixteen switchbacks. There was a gleam on Melissa's face. "I made it!" she said. "It's a wonderful feeling to be on top of a mountain, even in the rain."

"Just imagine what the view would be like on a clear day," said Mayo.

We continued on through Gathland State Park to Crampton Gap. At a small, but dry, shelter we crawled into our sleeping bags to get warm. Gayla laughed. "We're snug as three bugs in a rug, except there are five of us. Just listen to the rain! I'm glad to be in here."

On our last day we hiked through George Washington Memorial Park. "I'd like to come back to both parks when it isn't cloudy," said Mayo.

Melissa and Carol reached the car first. "I feel great!" Melissa said. "I never dreamed I could hike seventy-five miles and survive with so little."

Mayo wanted some books from Trail Headquarters, so we returned to Harpers Ferry. While the rest of the group shopped, I walked back to the A.T. and hiked the portion of the Trail we had skipped. The weather cleared, providing an impressive view of the little town of Harpers Ferry, situated

113

between the junction of the Potomac and Shenandoah Rivers. As we drove home, we talked about how much American history had taken place in this part of our country. We had learned about the Tow Canal, the little town of Harpers Ferry, and walked the same ground as George Washington.

CHAPTER TWELVE

Thumper and I furnished the transportation when we returned to New England. Bucket, Carmel and Carala were veterans. Bucket's sister Karen, Johanna, Dianna H., and Sonnie, an adult, were novices. Jeane H., who had hiked in the Smokies and now lived in Hanover, New Hampshire where our trek would end, had agreed to be our car shuttle person. We picked her up on our way to Gorham. The girls and I waited while Jeane and Thumper took my station wagon to Franconia Notch. When they returned, Jeane drove Thumper's car back to Hanover, 140 miles south. It was late and we had to hurry to make Rattle River Lean-to before dark.

Early in the morning we were all anxious to get started. Thumper was with the lead group; Sonnie and I were behind. Many trails cross the White Mountains. The lead group took the Trail to the summit of Mt. Mariah then somehow got onto the wrong trail. It was two o'clock before the group was together for lunch. Zeta Pass, where we planned to camp, was still a long way off, and everyone hurried over North Carter Mountain, taking a brief glance at the view of Wild River Valley and continued on to Mt. Lethe.

We came to open ledges on Mt. Lethe and I asked Sonnie, "Can you make it up the ledge with your pack on, or do you want to take it off and let me hand it to you after you're up?"

Sonnie decided to take off her pack, and I showed her where to put her foot and where to get a hand hold on the ledge. "I don't think I can do this," she quivered.

115

"Yes you can," I encouraged, "just pull hard with your hands."

She got up to the ledge and I handed her pack up. Before I made it up she had disappeared. At the next ledge, Sonnie was waiting. "I can make it here with my pack on," she told me.

"Let me go first and I'll pull you up," I suggested.

As soon as she was up, she moved quickly on while I stood a moment to admire the view. The same thing kept happening; I'd catch up and help her, and she'd race on to the next ledge. She was very uneasy about climbing on the ledges.

Before we reached the summit of Middle Carter Mountain, the wind was whipping the branches of the trees, and we could see an impending storm. We put our pack covers and ponchos on, but the wind slashed at our ponchos making them useless. The branches twisted in the hard wind and the rain, pouring down in sheets, was blown with such force that it stung our faces. At Zeta Pass, Karen and Bucket got water while the rest of us pitched the tents. It had been a long, steep, wet ten-mile day.

I was awakened early by a bird's song and went to the spring for water. It was eight o'clock before I returned and after nine before we left camp, a much later start than usual on a day when we had several steep mountains to climb. We reached Carter Notch Hut in cold rain and clouds. Carter Notch Hut is the first of the A.M.C. (Appalachian Mountain Club) huts, a unique chain of mountain hostels, providing meals, lodging, trail and weather information. Thumper met us as Sonnie and I walked into the hut. I asked, "Is everyone here?"

"Yes," she said, "but I have bad news. The people here say the weather is too bad to hike over Wildcat Mountain. They advise taking the Nineteen-Mile Trail to the road and catching a ride to Pinkham Notch."

"We'd better take their advice," I said, "I've heard the weather can be extremely dangerous on top of the mountains in the Presidential Range."

The group trotted down the Nineteen-Mile Trail to the road where some friendly tourists drove us to Pinkham Notch, the main headquarters for the hut system. The White Mountains were steep and rougher than any of us expected. Thumper asked the group if they'd be willing to add another day to our trek so that we could take it slower over the rough, rocky terrain. Our original plan was to skip Mizpah A.M.C. Hut, but after our first two days of hiking, the girls decided it would be better to stop and add an extra day. These arrangements would make it impossible to get to Hanover in time for Thumper to get back to work.

116

The weatherman reported it was safe to hike on the mountains, and Carmel and Bucket sped out. We climbed toward the summit of Mt. Madison with the girls scrambling like mountain goats from one big rock to another. Sonnie said, "I do fine on these rocks as long as there are trees around and I can't see how high I am, but when I come to an open space I'm terrified."

We were about 300 yards from being above the timberline of Mt. Madison, and I started preparing her for what it would be like. "Don't look from side to side," I told her, "just look straight down at your feet."

The sun was shining as we walked out of the trees. Sonnie was doing fine, but as we got closer to the top, she moved slower. Finally she stopped altogether. "I'm too scared to move," she said.

I moved slowly, hoping she would come on when she realized she was alone, but she didn't move. Then I called, "Come on if you can; it's going to rain," and she managed to force her legs to budge. I was anxious to get on top of the first peak, but before we could get there, the clouds blew in. The rain and clouds prevented Sonnie from seeing how high she was. Inching our way over the rocks across the top of the first peak and along the ridge following the cairn, we came to a big yellow sign warning of the danger of being on the mountains when the weather was bad. We also saw a sign to the Parapet Trail that contours the side of Mt. Madison and leads to Madison Hut. Not wanting Sonnie to get stuck on Mt. Madison, we took the Parapet Trail and arrived at Madison Hut just in time for supper. Thumper asked, "What took you so long?"

I answered, "Sonnie and I took the Parapet Trail. She's uncomfortable above the timberline. Crossing the Presidential Range is going to be very difficult for her."

"How did the girls do," I asked.

"Great," replied Thumper, "They had a ball. The clouds were so thick we could hardly see each other, but the blazes on the cairns were visible when the wind blew. We did have a little excitement though. Carmel looked up at the sky and asked, 'What is that? It looks like a big orange balloon.'"

"What was it?" I asked.

"My new pack cover. The wind caught it just right, tore it off my pack and blew it off the mountain," she laughed.

"So that's what it was," I chuckled, "I saw something strange flying through the sky down the mountain."

We had a delicious meal of stew, homemade bread and fresh green salad, then retired to our bunks and blankets. At the breakfast bell, hot, nourishing food was served. The standing joke with the hut people was "you'd better eat your farina, or it'll be in your bread tonight." The cooks used every bit of food carried up to the hut because if it wasn't eaten, they had to carry it down. After breakfast, the hut group put on a show demonstrating a special technique of folding the blankets, so they would be ready for the next group. Only a few people ran each hut, and they spent their time carrying and preparing food. The guests folded the blankets and readied the dormitory rooms for the next group of hikers.

The most exciting and challenging mountain of all was before us, Mt. Washington, 6,288 feet, the highest mountain north of the Carolinas and east of the Mississippi. We had read about storms arising with great rapidity and incredible violence, producing winds of hurricane force and freezing conditions even in summer. I had prayed, "Please don't let me get on this mountain with a group of girls and have a sudden weather change."

The sun was shining and there wasn't a cloud in the sky when we started toward the first ridge. We looked back to see Madison Hut resembling a doll house nestled among the barren mountains. Reaching the top of the ridge, we could see Mt. Madison at the side and Mt. Washington and the other mountains of the Presidential Range in front. We also saw little green and red packs that looked like specks moving along the trail and knew it was our group. There were cairn along the way, but with unlimited visibility we didn't need them. God had answered my prayer. It was a perfect day, making up for all the clouds on Katahdin, Avery Peak, and Bigelow Range. Sonnie raced ahead. I knew it was requiring every bit of courage she could muster. She wanted to get over the mountain as fast as possible, while I wanted to make the thrill of being here last as long as I could.

I found Thumper among the many tourists on the summit. She told me all the girls were there and that Sonnie had decided she couldn't take the height and was going to catch a ride down and go home.

Dianna came to me and said, "Can you believe the wind was blowing ninety-seven miles an hour here on the afternoon we had the thunderstorm on Carter Mountain. It blew over a huge equipment truck."

Karen came up and added, "I just read that the highest wind speed ever was recorded here."

Getting some snacks and telling Sonnie goodbye, we began the 1-5/10 mile trek down the mountain to Lake of the Clouds Hut. The hut was a little speck in the distance. At the hut I found the girls in a group chatting about the day's events. "Hiking on the rocks in the sunshine is fabulous! Did I get a suntan?" Carmel asked as she held out her arm.

"It's the most awesome hiking I've ever done," Dianna said, "and the views make me feel so tiny."

The following day we came to Mizpah Spring Hut. It was like being at a family reunion. Related through our backpacking and hiking, we had lots to talk about. One hiker asked Bucket why she was hiking the A.T..

"I've hiked before and wanted to see the White Mountains," she said, "I think it's the most exciting challenge for Girl Scouts."

"This is my first trip," Johanna added. "I wondered if I would make it, but Mama Boots' motto, 'one step at a time,' was a life saver. Backpacking is a real challenge. I can't believe I conquered Mt. Washington." She paused with a look of wonder on her face, "I still can't believe that view from the top of Mt. Washington."

Johanna later wrote about being above the timberline.

> The first time we walked above the timberline it was a very spooky and eerie feeling for me. Nothing to tower over me, all the bushes crouched at my feet. Everything seemed frozen in still life. As I thought about it, I realized this was the wind's space, and the wind said "I am boss here. You can stay if you want, but you have to live by my rules." So the trees got shorter and the flowers grew in small clumps out of protected cracks in the rocks. Soon, I was enjoying the wind blowing through my hair and against my face.

Carala hiked with me and asked some very interesting questions about religions and the history of the different faiths. I could only explain my feelings and how religion had affected my life. I suggested it would be a good research project for her when we returned home.

We walked on to an outcropping called Webster Cliffs and could see the rest of the group sitting on another outcropping far below. We yelled at them, and they heard us and waved. Climbing down to the group, everyone enjoyed lunch with a view straight down into Crawford Notch. We were at the top of a ladder created by nature.

Dianna and Carmel turned around backwards and carefully stepped from rocks to roots to rocks, grabbing at branches and saplings with their hands, as they eased themselves down the steep side to Crawford Notch. The rest of us watched closely, so we could use the same foot and hand holds.

119

The caretaker at Ethon Pond Lean-to assigned us two platforms for our tents. After supper, Dianna said, "I'm having a great time. I've never been this high before. I like hiking above the tree line. Coming down Webster Cliffs was a blast."

Bucket added, "I'd rather hike over the rocks than in the bogs in Maine where I wore out my shoes and kept losing them in the mud."

Carmel, a very sure-footed hiker, said, "I really enjoyed both trips, but I've got to admit it's nice to have dry feet."

Johanna complained, "I'd rather be at the huts than here. I don't like the bugs."

"Bugs?" scoffed Bucket, "These are nothing compared to the ones in Maine."

Karen, who wasn't too enthusiastic, said, "I'd rather be home watching TV."

Morning dawned a bright, sunny day. We stopped at a waterfall and watched the water cascade down the creek, enjoyed flowers along the trail and had a grand old time walking along an old railroad bed. We made it to Zealand Falls Hut by noon and spent the afternoon lying in the sun, mesmerized by the water going over the falls. A rainbow followed a late afternoon thunderstorm, as we watched from the hut porch.

On the summit of Mt. Guyot, Thumper told me her leg was hurting. She took some pain killers and continued along the ridge to the summit of South Twin Mountain, then descended to the base and immediately started the climb up Mt. Garfield. About halfway up, we came to Garfield campsite.

At daylight, we finished the steep ascend. Descending into a col, we began the climb of Mt. Lafayette. From the summit, we could see mountains, ridges, lakes and Greenleaf A.M.C. Hut, nestled in the rocks below. Over minor summits, still above the timberline, the Trail continued over Mt. Lincoln, where I overheard Carmel talking to Bucket.

"How can you explain to your friends how it feels to be on top of a mountain like this?" she asked. "There are no words to express it. You just have to experience it to know how it feels."

We rested in complete silence, observing the mountains and hoping the picture would forever remain captured in our minds. Between Mt. Lafayette and Mt. Lincoln was a view of Lonesome Lake and Hut, where we would be staying the next day. We made our way across the barren ridges and down to Liberty Springs campsite for the night.

Carmel and Bucket were again in the lead as we left for Franconia Notch. There we discovered someone had tried to break into the station wagon. The would-be thief had tried to pry the back door open. It was badly bent, but our food was safe. Several cars in the area had been vandalized.

Carmel heard about a small restaurant and said, "I sure would like a hamburger. Can we go to the restaurant for lunch?"

"I like the way you think," said Bucket.

We drove to the restaurant and sat at an outdoor picnic table eating hamburgers, french fries and milk shakes until we thought we would burst. "Mama Boots," Thumper said, "My leg is in so much pain I don't think I can hike any farther, and I don't think you should leave your car here. Would it be all right if I took the car to Hanover and stayed with Jeane until Wednesday? I could meet you in Glencliff with food for you and the girls hiking on and pick up the girls going home with me."

We talked it over with the girls and everyone agreed. We hiked on without Thumper toward Lonesome Lake A.M.C. Hut. The girls took a swim in the lake and canoed to a spot where they could see Mt. Lafayette, Mt. Lincoln and the ridges we had hiked silhouetting the horizon. One of the campers at the hut had a banjo. Carmel was an excellent banjo player and loved to play, so we spent the evening singing on the porch of the hut while she played.

The morning weather report predicted rain and clouds, but nothing severe. We were leaving the White Mountains and heading toward Vermont. To the summit of Kinsman Mountain, the trail was steep, wet, and rough. Descending to a creek with several waterfalls, we came to Eliza Brook Lean-to. The girls were ahead of me and were already stretched out resting. The brook ran right beside the lean-to, creating a very tranquil atmosphere with the water trickling around the rocks and down the mountain.

An end-to-ender had come in late and slept under the overhang of the lean-to. He was hiking north. Carmel said, "You'll have fun on the rocks in the White Mountains."

Bucket added, "Watch out for the bogs and bugs in Maine. Both will try to swallow you whole."

"I thought the Mahoosuc Notch was a blast," Carmel said. "It was great hopping from one huge rock to another." "I hope you have nice weather," I added. "The day we hiked Mount Washington was perfect."

By the time he left, he knew what to expect for the remainder of his trek. The trail descended into Kinsman Notch and on to Beaver Brook Shelter. This was the last night the group would be together. It was a nice group and they

were very compatible. I wondered if splitting the group was a wise thing to do. We wouldn't reach our goal of getting to Hanover, but we had hiked the number of days that we'd planned. The next morning we discussed what we should do. "How many want to continue to Hanover according to our original plan," I asked.

"I'd like to continue," Dianna said. "This may be my only chance to see this part of the country."

Bucket said, "I need to get home and get ready for school."

"Mama Boots," Carmel said, "you could start the next group at Glencliff. Dianna can come along on that trip, and I think my sister Theresa would like to hike then too."

When we reached Glencliff, Carmel told Thumper we were all going home together. "Are you sure the girls won't be disappointed at not reaching their goal?" Thumper asked me.

"I don't think so," I replied. "Dianna would like to continue, but the others feel they need to get home. We hiked the number of days we'd planned, just not the distance."

"Well," Thumper replied, "it looks like we did reach our goal of offering the girls a growing, learning experience."

"Yes," I said. "I know it's taught me a lot. I'm sorry they didn't get to hike Wildcat Mountain, but we couldn't do much about that, considering the weather. Maybe someday we'll try this trek again."

CHAPTER THIRTEEN

In July another group had decided to continue hiking south from Glencliff, New Hampshire. Erawanda K., a school bus driver, agreed to take us to Glencliff in her recreational vehicle. She and her husband, Marvin, would resupply our food halfway and pick us up at Highway 11. Dianna couldn't go even though she had planned to when we finished at Glencliff. Her sister Bobbie and Carmel's sister Theresa were our novice hikers and Carala, Harriet and Bucket wanted to add more A.T. miles to their record. Gayla had such a good time hiking in the Shenandoah National Park in April, she wanted to see what the Trail was like in New England.

The Trail crosses the road near Glencliff. Harriet said, "Let's hurry and get our sleeping bags on our packs. I can't wait to get started. You're going to like the feeling when you reach the top of the mountain," she told Bobbie.

Carala added, "I love the peaceful evenings, and I can't wait to see the Green Mountains."

Bucket chimed in, "I'm glad to get away from the hustle and bustle at home."

At our first lean-to, Gayla returned giggling from a visit to the latrine and said, "When I reached the end of the blue blazes, there sat a box on a concrete platform with two footprints in the cement. Deciding this had to be a practical joke, I looked for some more blue blazes but there weren't any. Then I looked around for the practical joker. I just knew as soon as I started to sit down one would pop out from behind a tree and say, 'Ha, I fooled you.' I noticed someone walking a short distance away and decided he was on the trail. I thought, this can't be the privy, there are no sides and no top, no privacy at all. But out of desperation I sat down. No one popped out to surprise me, but I didn't linger on that box in wide open space. The Dartmouth Outing Club must have figured it would always be dark when hikers used this privy."

We had a good laugh and were well prepared for the unusual privy. Everyone was in good spirits, tired but proud of our long day. It was great to have such a witty group.

Theresa, Harriet, and Bucket were the first to start the climb up Smart Mountain. We hiked all day, eating red raspberries along the trail. When we reached the lean-to, I checked out the latrine. It was like the other one except it had a view of the ridges, valley, and mountains, and was set in a clump of trees. Carala questioned, "Why don't they put sides on the latrine?"

"Maybe it's hard to bring wood in here to build a building," Bucket suggested.

Bobby remarked, "At least they don't smell bad."

"I bet that's the reason for leaving them open," Theresa said, "The rain washes them, the wind blows the odor away and the sunshine kills the germs."

The shelter was an older one. Rain blew in the front, water ran down the sides, and the roof leaked. We put a tent rain-fly across the front and our ponchos over us, but it was a miserable night.

At Trapper John Lean-to, there were four end-to-enders. Two were from New Zealand, one from Wisconsin, whose trail name was "Bullwinkle," and one from Maryland called "Rockie." Theresa and Harriet asked the young men from New Zealand about trails there. They made comparisons but said, "There's no trail in New Zealand quite like the A.T.."

We stopped in Hanover to replenish our food supplies and crossed the Connecticut River to Vermont. After a night at Happy Hill Cabin, we followed the Trail across farmland between the Connecticut River and the Green Mountains. Vic, an end-to-ender, told Harriet and Theresa about a little store along the road that had ice cream and about a nice place to swim in the White River. We sat on the steps of the store eating a half-gallon of ice cream. At the White River we found a big rope dangling from a limb. The water looked inviting, but the morning air was too cool, so we continued through overgrown pastures.

Sherri asked, "Isn't it about time for lunch? There's a big tree over there with lots of shade. Let's eat."

Under a big Vermont sugar maple, we ate lunch then started the climb up Thistle Hill. Theresa said, "I wish we were back at the White River and could take a cool swim."

The trail traversed open slopes and abandoned farmland. Although Bobbie had been ahead of me when I arrived at the lean-to, she wasn't there. I asked Jennifer and Bruce, a couple camping at the junction of the trail, "Did you see a girl pass by?"

Jennifer said, "I saw someone pass about fifteen minutes ago."

I asked, "Did she have a blue hat and a red pack?"

"Yes," said Bruce. "Jennifer and I will catch her."

As we waited for Jennifer and Bruce to return with Bobbie, the girls put up tents. The lean-to was old and infested with bugs. According to the trail register, there were porcupine around. The little bugs must have been carried in by the porcupine.

Mid-morning we came to a HIKERS WELCOME sign. Harriet stopped and said, "The blazes go that way on the road, but the sign points in the opposite direction into the woods."

Theresa looked around and asked, "Isn't that a blaze on the side of that old barn? It's not as bright as the ones on the road."

"Carala, get the guidebook," I suggested.

According to the book, we should turn right, into the woods. We followed the old blazes and the guidebook, figuring there must have been some rerouting of the Trail. A short distance through the woods, we crossed a fence into a pasture and then came to a road. Along the road there was a big patch of black raspberries which appeared to have been intentionally mowed around and left for hikers. Dragging ourselves out of the raspberries, we made our way to the Gulf Lean-to. Four end-to-enders were there. Since we were traveling in the opposite direction on the trail, we were like a communication line.

Bob asked, "Have you seen Pete? I got off the trail for food supplies, and I wondered how far ahead of me he is."

Harriet replied, "I remember talking to a guy from Virginia named Pete. Would that be him?"

Frank asked about John, and Bucket told the end-to-enders about the bogs in Maine. Harriet added stories about the White Mountains and asked Emily and Tom, a married couple, "Why are you hiking the trail?"

Emily replied, "We're tired of being librarians. We resigned from our jobs, sold our house and are hiking the A.T. to give ourselves time to think and evaluate what we really want to do."

The group climbed to an overlook and the site of an old fire tower where we found a large plastic jar filled with water and a trail register. The Barnards, whose property we were on, kept the water and register there for the hikers. Theresa took off her shoes to relax her feet and said, "The people in Vermont are sure hospitable, with the water jug here, the raspberries we found and the man who welcomes hikers on his property."

Bucket said, "It's been really nice hiking in Vermont. There haven't been any strenuous climbs, and it's really been relaxing."

After a long rest and view of the Ottauquechee Valley and Green Mountains, we pulled ourselves away and came to Stony Brook Lean-to. Porcupines had gnawed the seat of the latrine. We wondered which was worse, a box with no building or a building with no seat? We were awakened during the night by a porcupine gnawing on the shelter. Theresa turned on her flashlight, and we watched the little quills bobbing up and down just outside the lean-to.

We were to meet Erawanda and Marvin for our new supply of food, showers, and clean clothes, so we wasted no time in the morning. We hiked on abandoned logging roads, looking at the distant mountains. Gayla said, "We'll soon be climbing mountains again. Those must be the Green Mountains"

North of Sherburne Pass, the Trail ascended to its junction with the Long Trail, and we hurried down to the Long Trail Lodge. Erawanda fixed sausage and eggs in the RV for breakfast. What a welcome change from oats! Packing our clean clothes and new supply of food, we started hiking in a downpour. By noon we came to Cooper Lodge, located below Killington Peak, the second highest mountain in Vermont.

At Governor Clement Memorial Shelter, Theresa and Bucket built a fire in the fireplace to warm the damp air. While I was gathering wood, I found the latrine. It had a plaque which read, "Lieut. Gov. Jarvis Snodgrass Memorial Gazebo." The trail club didn't want to leave out the lieutenant governor.

We were now on the last third of our hike, and everyone was doing fine. The trail wound through wilderness terrain densely forested with evergreens in the higher elevations, and northern hardwood trees in lower areas.

We stopped for lunch by the Bob Brugmann Bridge, built in memory of a seventeen year old end-to-ender who lost his life while crossing the flooded Mills River on a log in the Clarendon Gorge. The gorge is narrow with very steep walls. A year and a half after Bob's tragic drowning, the new bridge was dedicated, and now we could hike across in complete safety. Ascending steeply out of the gorge, we had hiked 13-6/10 miles when we reached Greenwall Shelter.

Our day began by hiking through a very scenic part of the Green Mountains with lots of cabins and shelters for tourists. We had walked on split logs to protect the delicate vegetation of the marsh land and bog before, but around Little Rock Pond we walked on split logs all the way. We crossed the road and started toward Lost Pond Shelter, our goal for the day.

Everyone was ready for our last full day of hiking, up Baker Peak and down through hardwood forest to Griffith Lake. We found a sign informing us that Mad Tom Shelter had been moved a mile and a half farther on.

Carala and Bucket were first to leave on our last five miles. The rest of us climbed up Bromley Mountain, right behind them. The Trail followed a ski run down the other side. When we arrived at the parking lot, Carala and Bucket weren't there. I was concerned since they had started first. The girls started changing their shoes for the ride home, and I was debating what to do, when Carala and Bucket walked in. They had hiked up to see the Alpine Chairlift and visited with some other hikers we had met earlier on the trail.

Sitting in the parking lot waiting for Erawanda, Bobbie was doctoring her blisters. "It's sure great that this trip is finished," she said. "I'm glad I came, but I don't think I'll ever do anything like this again. I may just drop out of Scouts."

"I knew you were hiking slowly, but I didn't know you were having problems," I said.

"I don't like doing the things they do in Girl Scouts," she answered, "I joined because Dianna likes it, and I came on this trip because she likes back-packing."

"I came because my sisters like it, but I found out I like it too," Theresa added. "I enjoy being a Girl Scout. We do all kinds of neat projects—camping, service projects and just plain fun. I've gotten into planning what my troop is doing. If you get involved in planning, it gives you a say in what you do."

Erawanda and Marvin drove into the parking lot, and we packed our things into the RV for the trip home. We recounted the new friends we'd made and congratulated each other on completing 135 miles of the A.T.. We had finished the State of New Hampshire, hiked in Vermont and learned the difference between the White Mountains and the Green Mountains.

*   *   *   *   *

Harriet and Theresa spearheaded the trip back to New England. Karen B., who had hiked in Virginia, joined them, and I called Dianna. Other commit-

128

ments prevented her from going this time also. A couple of days later Bobbie called and said she'd like to go on this trip. Surprised, I asked, "Are you still registered as a Girl Scout?"

"No," she answered, "Do I have to be?"

"Yes, Bobbie, participants are all supposed to be involved with scouting," I replied.

"If I register now, will that count?" she asked. "I was in scouting last year."

"Can you come to the planning meetings and do all the exercises required before the hike?" I asked. "Remember, last time you had a hard time keeping up."

Bobbie agreed to do all the extra walking and step climbing that were a part of conditioning, and to come to our planning meetings. At our first session, Theresa looked surprised to see Bobbie and said, "I thought you didn't like backpacking."

"I changed my mind," she answered. "I'm going to try hard to get in condition and maybe this time I won't get those big blisters."

Johanna was also in the group of five girls with Gayla and me. Starting the meeting, Harriet said, "I'd like to be able to say I've hiked the whole state of Massachusetts in one trip. There are only eighty-eight miles of trail in that state, so we could begin at Route 11 in Vermont and hike south through Massachusetts to Route 44 in Connecticut." The others agreed, and we went on to make the rest of our plans.

Erawanda and Marvin dropped us off at the Vermont Highway 11 parking lot, and we were off on another 110 miles of the A.T.. Our first day of hiking had no major climbs, and the last mile was around Stratton Pond to Bigelow Shelter, located on the shore of the pond. Two end-to-enders, Morgan from New Jersey, and Tallahassee Tom from Florida, came by the shelter to fix their supper. Tom said, "I wondered if we'd catch you."

I was confused and asked, "Have we met before?"

Tom asked, "Aren't you the group whose picture was in the photo album at Harpers Ferry?"

"Yes and no," I answered, "I was in that picture, but this is a different group of girls. This is our first night on the trail. We started at Route 11."

The next morning, Karen was crying. I asked, "What's the problem?"

She said, "I want to go home."

I questioned her. "Are you sick?"

She said, "No, I just want to go home."

I told her, "I don't have any way to send you home. You'll just have to bite the bullet and hike."

I felt mean, but I knew her parents wouldn't want me to send her home unless there was a good reason. We trekked on following the Trail in southern Vermont and spent the night at Kid Gore Shelter.

We came to an abandoned fire tower that had been renovated by the Forest Service to make an observation deck for hikers. "Oh, I wish I had my paints," Karen said, "I'd love to paint this scene."

"It is pretty up here, isn't it?" I responded, "Aren't you glad you stayed?"

"Oh, yes," she said, with a smile that spoke for itself.

Leaving the fire tower deck, Harriet and Theresa stopped to talk to a group of ladies who called themselves "old" Girl Scouts. They were from New York and were hiking north. We talked for quite a while and compared Girl Scouting in New York and Kentucky. Both groups wished we were going in the same direction so we could continue the conversation.

Melville Nauheim Shelter really looked good after 12-5/10 miles of hiking. After breakfast, we started descending and crossed the William A. MacArthur Memorial Bridge. The bridge was a good place to watch the rushing water with its many ripples and small cascades coming from between the trees and rushing under the bridge. The trail crossed Bennington-Battleboro Highway and started a very steep climb on rock and log steps. Karen counted the steps as she climbed. When we reached the summit of Harmon Hill Karen had counted 1,452 steps. Her spirits were much improved.

While the girls were fixing supper, a hiker came in with a bag full of mushrooms he had picked. He was preparing the mushrooms while Karen and Harriet cooked our supper. They placed a chocolate pie in the center of the picnic table. The hiker offered us some of his mushrooms, but no one would accept them. Finally he said, "I can't stand this any longer. Can I have a piece of your pie?"

The girls, laughing with pride, gave him a piece of the pie. Crossing the Vermont-Massachusetts border we ascended Greylock Mountain, the highest in Massachusetts and spent the next night in Bascom Lodge, where Harriet and Theresa heard that the community center in Dalton, Massachusetts welcomed hikers and provided hot showers.

Dalton was sixteen miles away, so we hurried down the mountain through the town of Cheshire, Massachusetts past Gore and Anthony Ponds and on to the center. As the afternoon wore one, Bobbie kept getting slower and slower, and we were all quite tired when we arrived at the community center. After supper and showers, we slept on mats placed on the floor for the hikers.

The next campsite with water was fourteen-miles down the Trail. Bobbie was still very tired, and we all doubted our ability to hike that far. We had hiked about an hour when Bobbie threw down her pack and said, "I'm going home."

I replied, "You can't go home. There's no transportation, and even if there were, I left the money with Erawanda."

Bobbie snapped, "I've got fifty dollars. I'll find a way home."

"Your sister," I began.

"I'm not Dianna," she yelled as she took food and a part of the tent out of her pack, "Why does everybody insist I have to like everything she likes and do everything she does?"

"I'm sorry, Bobbie. Please wait," I said, "you shouldn't go off by yourself. Won't you please change your mind?"

She neither looked back nor said another word. I hiked slowly on, thinking she would change her mind when she realized she was on her own. Around a bend, just out of sight, the other girls were waiting. Harriet said, "Mama Boots, you can't let her go back by herself."

I replied, "I can't carry her. I tried to get her to stay with us but she wouldn't. Let's wait a while. Maybe she'll change her mind."

We ate blackberries growing along the trail and waited. Harriet asked, "Why did Bobbie come on this trip? She had so much trouble last year."

"Maybe she just wanted to get away from home," I said, "I'd called Dianna and she wanted to come but couldn't. Then Bobbie called and said she wanted to come."

Harriet sighed. "Well, Bobbie just thought she wanted to come because Dianna likes backpacking. But Bobbie just doesn't seem to have 'green blood' like Dianna."

I could tell Harriet was really worried and said, "This is one of those times you have to have faith that she'll be all right. It's the way parents feel when their children decide to go out on their own. It hurts, but there isn't much you can do about it."

Reaching a cascade of water, we stopped for lunch. It was only a short distance to October Shelter, so we filled the water bag and carried it to the shelter. Worried about Bobbie, we really didn't feel like hiking any farther. We hoped that maybe she was trying to catch us.

The next day, we found a telephone where the Trail crossed a road. I called Papa and asked him to call Bobbie's parents. He called back after a few minutes and reported she'd gotten home safely. "I feel Bobbie has had a learning experience from this," I told the group, "Bobbie has always been compared to Dianna and tried to do everything Dianna did because she thought that was expected of her. I think Bobbie has learned more about herself and can now begin to establish her own identity."

Harriet said, "That's one reason I like backpacking. It gives me a chance to learn about myself."

Relieved that Bobbie had made it home, we went on to Upper Goose Pond. Harriet put on a one person act that she had used at camp. She squeezed her face up and said, "My name is Chubby. My mother is chubby, my brother is chubby and even my goldfish is chubby. My Mother said, 'You are so chubby I bet you can't smile.' Yes, I can." With that, Harriet tried to smile with her face all pushed up. We laughed, relieving the tension of the day.

We crawled into our tents to wait out the storm. We all had the giggles. No matter what was said, everyone laughed. When the rain stopped, Gayla and Theresa started fixing supper. Johanna and Karen, who was really getting into the spirit of backpacking, were fixing Kool Aid when we heard someone talking with a southern accent. He came over and introduced himself as Ron Keal, the caretaker for the Goose Pond area. I asked, "Where are you from?"

He replied, "Vine Grove, Kentucky."

I told him we were from Louisville and he asked, "Are you Mama Boots?"

I answered, "Yes, how did you know?"

He smiled, "I was hiking the trail from Georgia to Maine, about four days from Katahdin, and met a lady who was hiking the trail in small trips with Girl Scouts. The girls called her 'Mama Boots.' I figure you're the same lady."

"Yes," I replied, "I'm still at it."

Ron noticed Harriet's W.K.U. t-shirt and said, "I graduated from Western Kentucky University. Are you a student there?"

Harriet replied, "Yes, I've one more year. Would you explain your job of caretaker? I may be looking for a job next summer."

Ron explained, "I keep an eye on the activities around the pond so that no one camps or builds fires in a restricted area. I do maintenance on the trail when I've time. I live over on the other side of the pond. Would you like to see my cabin?"

We had finished eating, so Harriet, Johanna and Karen went with Ron while Gayla, Theresa, and I cleaned up supper dishes. When they returned, they were giggling, telling Gayla and Theresa all about the experience. Ron had told them where there was a secluded place to take a swim. On the way back from his cabin, they stopped and Harriet and Johanna took a skinny dip. Karen stood guard but a man and his son, canoeing on the pond, interrupted their swim. The good news that Bobbie had gotten home, renewing old friendships, and having a fun evening gave me a grateful feeling.

While we were eating breakfast, Ron returned to say goodbye, and we told him we were stopping at Tyingham to pick up our food package. We were putting the food into our packs when Ron walked up with two half-gallons of ice cream and some cookies. What a treat! We sat on the post office steps and ate it all.

Our last full day of the trek, we climbed the steep cliff of Jud End Mountain, over Mt. Everett and Race and crossed the Massachusetts-Connecticut state line. The deciduous trees were beginning to turn to fall colors, giving us a sneak preview of the vivid colors a few weeks from now. We climbed Bear Mountain, the highest mountain in Connecticut and on to Brassie Brook Lean-to.

At sunup, we hurried to finish the last four miles of the trek. Erawanda and Marvin picked us up about nine-thirty, and we were on our way home. Harriet interrupted my thoughts saying, "Mama Boots, this will probably be my last trip with you. Next summer I'll be working, since I graduate in May."

"Oh, I'll surely miss you. We've had a lot of fun over the past five years. The first trip was when we turned back in Georgia because of snow. We were together for five weeks in Europe and three hiking trips in New England. Write down your feelings about hiking so I can keep them in my file."

Harriet wrote:

> My clearest memory of hiking is of thinking this is never going to end, then feeling regret when we had finished the trek. Someday I'd like to hike the complete trail. I'll always remember the long conversations I had with whomever I was hiking with. Our subjects—conservation, pollution, religion and boys—always seemed deeper than usual. I developed a respect for the earth's natural beauty. At the end of a day, I felt dog-tired, filthy dirty, stinky and great all at the same time. Most of all, I felt proud of myself, anxious to share my experience with my family and friends and sorry I couldn't go further. I now feel I'm a "can do" type person because of the "must do" experiences of the A.T..

I noticed Karen's constant smile and asked, "Aren't you glad you stayed with us?"

"I sure am," she replied. "I loved the scenery, but most of all I liked meeting new people. It's fun to work with a group. I don't feel as shy as I did."

Theresa interrupted, "Mama Boots, can I start planning the next trip? I'd like to continue south from Route 44. Someday I'd like to say I've hiked the Trail in bits and pieces."

"Great idea, Theresa," I replied.

*　　*　　*　　*　　*

A year later Theresa, along with Sherri, a Virginia hiker, and Jean S., our only first-time hiker, organized a hike from Connecticut Route 44 south to the Hudson River. My daughter Diane arranged to use her vacation time to go hiking with us.

We traveled to the home of Laura Atwood in Falls Village, Connecticut. Laura was going to help with our car shuttle. She put us on the trail at U.S. 44 where we'd finished last year.

First the trail crossed open fields, then crossed a brook and descended steeply alongside a high, wide waterfall. "This must be where the town of Falls Village got its name," Jean said.

Climbing Barrack Mountain, we sat on the peak, huffing and puffing. "This is the hardest climbing I've ever done," Jean said, panting.

"It'll get easier as we get used to the change from low altitudes and air conditioning," Theresa assured her.

With only slight changes in altitude, the Trail followed old roads through mature woods of pine, spruce and hemlock, with the spicy aroma of evergreens adding to our pleasure.

In the early morning sunlight of the third day, we walked through mature pine plantations. For a half mile we were in an extraordinary stand of huge, mature Cathedral Pines. Every sound and footfall was absorbed into silence by the thick carpet of pine needles. It was like being in church. Not a word was said as we moved through the pines, and we later agreed that we'd truly had a "closer walk with God."

In misty rain, we climbed the steep, rocky, almost vertical rise known as St. John's Ledges, and on up Cobbie and Chase Mountains with views of the Housatonic Valley. We circled around Macedonia Brook State Park and reached

135

Chase Mountain Lean-to in a hard rain. Finding no potable water, we hiked on into Kent.

With hair stuck to our faces, clothes dripping and boots caked with mud, we looked like drowned rats. I asked myself, "What is a fifty-five year old woman doing in a mess like this?" At the first service station we came to, I told the attendant, "I'm leader of a group of Girl Scouts, and we're looking for a dry place to sleep."

"You can use the garage at the back of the station," he offered. I rushed to the post office before it closed to get our food box. When I returned to the service station, the attendant took Diane to the Pizza Hut for carry-out, a real relief from our usual trail suppers of canned chicken and noodles. It had been a long, wet thirteen-mile day. The night passed with only one interruption; a confused skunk appeared inside the garage and had to be evicted—very carefully.

It was still raining the next day as we crossed the New York-Connecticut border and continued on to spend the night at the Wiley (Webstuck) Shelter about a half mile off the trail. I was the first to leave in the morning, and when I returned to the trail, I went the wrong direction for the first time since I'd started hiking. When Theresa didn't catch me she figured something was wrong. Though I was hiking as fast as I could, she was halfway down the mountain looking for me. We laughed when we got together. Theresa said, "Wait a few years before you repeat Connecticut. Let's do New York today."

We spent a good part of the day walking on the road and finally reached the Edward R. Murrow Memorial Park to camp for the night. Nick, a "bits and pieces" hiker from Texas, told us about Ralph's Cabin, about sixteen miles away, which had been donated to be used by hikers. He suggested we stay there because he'd heard the camping spots around New York were not very good. Sixteen miles sounded like a long way, but we decided to go for it. The trip involved a lot of road walking before the trail entered the high meadow of Stormville Mountain where we had a panoramic view of the Shawangunk and Catskill Mountains. We stopped late in the afternoon to rest, and Jean asked, "How much farther?"

"I don't know, Jean, but it shouldn't be far. Are you getting tired?"

"Yes, but it's much too rocky to camp here," she responded.

I had to agree. The southern slope of Stormville Mountain was quite rocky, and between the terrain and the heat, we were beginning to wonder if getting to the cabin would be worth it. Then the Trail crossed the Taconic State Parkway,

136

and just beyond was Ralph's Cabin. Ralph greeted us with cold watermelon and took Diane to a nearby store for ice cream.

Hikers had planted a garden the past spring, and Ralph told us we could see if there was anything to harvest. Theresa and I found tomatoes, beans and corn for a delightful meal.

During supper Ralph told us about a monastery twenty miles away that had opened a part of their building for hikers, we could sleep in beds with sheets, have hot showers and all the food we could eat. I thought this would be much too far for my group to hike but they were eager and willing to try.

At dawn we ate the doughnuts and fruit that Ralph had left for us and were hiking by six-thirty. The Trail ascended a mountain with a view of a lake, but we didn't stop for long. At the beginning of a long stretch of road hiking, the girls stopped and exchanged their hiking boots for light, soft-soled shoes. Sherri and I fell behind and hadn't seen the others since lunch. By four o'clock we were dripping with sweat, our stomachs were growling, and we still had miles to go.

Around six o'clock, we caught Diane, Theresa and Jean and started up the hill to Graymoor Monastery. Dinner was being served as we arrived, so we were shown our rooms and invited to come and eat. A cookout was in progress, complete with a pig on a spit. There was barbecued chicken, ribs, chunks of pork, corn on the cob, salad, watermelon and soft drinks. We were almost too tired to eat, but the meal was worth the trip.

After supper we took showers and went to bed. I couldn't sleep. I hadn't changed to light shoes for the road hike, and my feet throbbed all night. This was the longest hiking day we'd ever spent on the A.T..

We thought we were dreaming when we saw breakfast—pancakes, sausage, orange juice and real coffee. We ate heartily, thanked the people at the monastery and left to hike the remaining five miles to our station wagon parked at Bear Mountain Inn.

"How did you like hiking on the A.T.?" Theresa asked Jean as we drove along.

Jean thought a moment. "At first I was frustrated and wondered what I'd gotten myself into, but the scenery was so spectacular I forgot to worry about climbing mountains. Now that it's over, I'll miss it," she said. Then she wrinkled up her nose. "I won't miss that freeze-dried food and the 'Hershey squirts,' though."

Theresa laughed. "I'll agree with you, there. I want to hike again next year, though."

137

"I want to go again too," said Jean. "It's sure a good way to get to know yourself and other people. And it makes me believe in my own abilities too."

As we drew near the end of this ambitious A.T. adventure, I reflected on my own favorite memories of the 106 mile trip—the inspiring walk among cathedral pines, the rainy hike to Kent, the endless hike to Ralph's cabin, and the eagerness with which my dauntless group tackled our longest hike, forever to be known as "the twenty-mile day."

CHAPTER FOURTEEN

While working on a trail at a Kentuckiana Council camp, Sherri asked, "Have you hiked the whole trail?"

"No," I answered, "but if Theresa keeps organizing trips, I'll soon make it."

Sherri remarked, "I've always had a good time hiking. It's hard work, but that's part of the excitement."

"Would you like to go on the next A.T. trip?" I asked.

"I'd like to hike somewhere you haven't hiked," Sherri said. "I think it'd be great if you hiked the complete trail."

Sherri and I began plans to hike in Pennsylvania. DeAnna, Bev, Stephannie, and Caren joined the group as first time hikers, and Diane took her vacation in June to go with us. From the Delaware Water Gap, where the Delaware River forms the border between Pennsylvania and New Jersey, we would hike seventy-eight miles south to Port Clinton, Pennsylvania.

The Presbyterian Church of the Mountain maintains some rooms as a hostel for hikers and Jim, one of the members, helped us with the car shuttle. An end-to-ender, known as "Trailwalker," from Athens, Georgia, was also at the hostel. This was the first time these girls had met an end-to-ender. "Trailwalker" shared his Trail adventures, and the girls taught him some games to share with other hikers along the trail.

Stephannie, a thin, short girl, who looked like a pack with legs, fell and hurt her wrist the first day. As I wrapped her wrist she said, "It hurts, but I don't need my wrist to hike."

Among blooming Mountain Laurel, we found a blue-blazed trail leading to water and decided to camp. The blooms don't have a sweet scent like some flowers, but when you're surrounded by them the air has a fresh aroma. We had hiked ten miles over rocks. Pennsylvania's rocks have sharp points which stick up in the trail. If you step on the rock, the point sticks in the sole of your shoe and trips you; if you try to avoid the points by stepping between the rocks, they grab the sides of your boot and turn your ankles. The butcher rocks, as they are sometimes called, are a real challenge.

Camping high in the mountains, secluded in the wilderness, was a new experience for some of the girls. Caren said, "I wonder if there are any bears around here?"

"I hope not," Bev replied, "These tents wouldn't be much protection from a big animal."

"Let's put our packs in the tents," suggested Stephannie.

I hadn't been paying much attention to their conversation but my alarm-bell suddenly went off. Thinking of mice, I said, "Don't do that, the food will attract animals."

Later they told Diane they had cried but didn't want me to know they were afraid.

Joe and Al, two friends of Diane, met us at Wind Gap to hike with us on Saturday and Sunday. Saturday was filled with lots of chatting and fun as we meandered across the butcher rocks. Sunday it started raining before dawn and rained all day. The girls were very agreeable when I suggested, "Instead of putting up wet tents in this downpour, let's see if we can find a town and a drier place to stay."

The guidebook mentioned a small hotel in Danielsville. No one was there when we arrived, so Diane and I asked around, trying to find a dry place to sleep. Diane found Donna and Bob Price, who ran the hotel. They didn't have a room large enough, so they let us stay in their recreation room. Bob took Al and Joe back to their car at Wind Gap. Donna took Diane and Caren to a laundromat to dry our sleeping bags and wash our muddy, wet clothes. DeAnna and I spread the tents and ponchos to dry by the fire Donna had built in the fireplace.

In the morning, Bob drove us the mile and a half up the road to the trail before he went to work. It was damp but the sun was shining. When the group stopped to rest, Sherri and Stephannie were missing. I retraced the Trail calling "Tongo" for quite a distance, but there was no answer. I walked and called for another twenty minutes before I heard a faint distant "Tongo." When we were back together, Sherri said, "The marks on the rocks were white, and we were talking, then all of a sudden there was no trail. Nothing but big rocks going down the side of the mountain."

Stephannie joined in, "We didn't know what to do. It was impossible to follow the blazes; we were lost. Sherri started back up the mountain and I followed. I was scared we'd never find you all."

Sherri continued, "When we got back up the mountain to the trail, I realized we had followed the Game Land boundary markings, but I wondered if we'd ever catch up. When I heard you yelling, 'Tongo,' I screamed back as loud as I could. It sure was a relief to hear your voice and know we weren't lost anymore."

Later in the day as we were hiking in an open area, we came to a big boulder field. The white blazes went straight down over the boulders. "Oh, my gosh," I said, "This reminds me of Hunt's Spur coming down Katahdin in Maine."

We were partway down when the Trail turned, and we literally crawled around a rocky spur of the mountain. Grasping the huge rock with our finger tips, we cautiously scooted our feet along a narrow ledge in the side of the rock that was as big as a house. Fortunately Stephannie's wrist was much better. Once over the spur, we quickly descended the rest of the mountain, crossed a road and began a steady climb to George W. Outerbridge Lean-to where there was an extended view of the Lehigh Valley.

The butcher rocks and big rock boulder fields, or outcroppings, were very hard on our feet, but Mountain Laurel bloomed everywhere to distract us. Then something new occurred. The sun was shining, but a noise in the trees sounded like rain and little green drops fell. "This is gross," said Stephannie.

"Anybody have an umbrella?" asked Sherri, "This icky stuff keeps hitting me in the face."

"Oh yuck," said Bev, "Mama Boots what is this?"

"It's the doo-doo from the gypsy moths," I said, "I sure hope the foresters find a safe way to control these little worms."

In some places it looked like mid-winter; there wasn't a green leaf anywhere. The girls cooked with a poncho over the stove to keep our food clean, and we quickly got in our tents.

141

Camping is not allowed in the Hawk Mountain Sanctuary or the Hamburg Watershed, but the next shelter was too close. Where there was a spring and water, no camping was allowed; where camping was allowed, there was no water. At last we came to potable water and filled our canteens and water bag. We would have to carry the water until we found a place to camp. A north-bound end-to-ender named Mike told us about a site.

As soon as the tents were up, it started raining. After carrying water and preparing for dry camp, we had water from the heavens. The rain stopped long enough for Diane and Caren to fix supper, while Stephannie and Bev held a poncho over the stove to keep the gypsy moth do doo out of the food. "Why are there so many of these moths?" Stephannie asked. "Where's the balance of nature? Don't they have any enemies?"

"I don't know," Diane replied. "The balance must be way off because these critters sure have taken over."

The thunder in the distance came closer and closer. "If this is a dry camp, I'd sure hate to see a wet one," quipped Bev.

The water bag had enough potable water left for breakfast, and the weather looked good as we left on our last full day of the trek. Crossing a road, we had a long steep climb and met our first girl end-to-ender, Jennifer from Maine, hiking by herself. She told us not to miss the view from Pinnacle Point.

Our group had passed a lot of overlooks without stopping, but we were glad we didn't skip this one. It was 1,635 feet above a valley that looked like a giant patchwork quilt. Fields of different shades of green and yellow, lilliputian farm houses, barns, lakes, and rolling hills as far as we could see to the south, east, and west. This had to be the place that the hymn writer was thinking about when he wrote, "When I look down from lofty mountains grandeur—and feel the gentle breeze." We stayed to watch the shadow of the clouds slowly move across the valley, until we had to pull ourselves away to trek on to Windsor Furnace Lean-to.

Finishing the five miles to Port Clinton, we packed the car and traveled to Harpers Ferry, West Virginia, where we visited Trail Headquarters and bought A.T. t-shirts. We had learned about the sharp-pointed butcher rocks, the outstanding views of Pennsylvania and the devastating gypsy moth.

* * * * *

DeAnna, Stephannie, Johanna and Caren returned to hike south from Port Clinton to Churchtown, Pennsylvania, a distance of ninety miles, in June. Lisa

142

was a new trekker as was Carol M., an adult leader. Joe, a friend from last summer's trip in Pennsylvania, met us to help with the car shuttle. Caren and Johanna had a crush on Joe. Johanna said, "He's the most handsome man I've ever seen."

We set up tents in the camping area of a nearby park for the night and started our trek at daybreak. All the girls were fast hikers, leaving me trailing behind them. I came upon what I thought was a black snake, but when I approached, it shook its tail. It was the second snake I had seen that day. Catching up with the girls when they stopped to rest, I cautioned them to watch for snakes as we made our way to Neys Shelter.

We were off in a hurry at sunrise. The weather was hot, and the girls had heard about a swimming hole near our campsite for the night. They overexerted themselves and by lunch time were in a bad mood. Carol, who was keeping up with the girls, said, "The girls have been bickering all morning!"

"It seems personality day is arriving a bit early," I said, "They're trying to hike too fast in this heat. A swim this evening will calm them down."

We came to the swimming hole with a rope hung from a tree where we could swing out over a small lake and drop into the water. Although the water was cold, it was fun and refreshing and the mood of the group improved.

The third day of the trek would be short, but the group was again in a hurry. There seemed to be some unfriendly competition to see who could hike the fastest. While the Trail wasn't steep, it had the sharp-pointed butcher rocks and was overgrown with prickly blackberry vines. The A.T. in the south has its bald, grassy mountains and high altitude; Virginia has its long narrow ridges. New England has bogs and rocky steep climbs to reach the summits above the timberline, and Pennsylvania has rocks. The rocks, given names by the hikers, such as devil rocks, butcher rocks, or spiny rocks, give the Trail in Pennsylvania its unique identity.

I didn't catch the girls until eleven o'clock. Stephannie met me and said, "Caren was going to find a tree and stepped into a hole and hurt her knee."

"How bad?" I asked.

"There's a big knot on her knee," Carol explained, "I've wrapped it with an Ace bandage, but she's in pain and can't walk. I think it should be X-rayed. Lisa and I will go for help."

As Lisa and Carol took off to find a way to get Caren to medical care, I gave Carol the keys to the car, saying, "The insurance papers are in the car."

I stayed with the group, and we found a place to camp. Caren said, "I can go to Joe's house until you all finish hiking."

143

Johanna responded, "If you go to Joe's house, I'm going with you."

We waited about two hours before we heard a vehicle coming down the abandoned dirt road. It was an old army jeep which the girls immediately called the "MASH unit jeep." Carol and Lisa were not with the jeep. There was no other adult to leave with the girls, so we all crammed into the "MASH unit jeep" with Caren. I asked the driver, "Where's the other leader and girl?"

He replied, "They gave us directions and said they were going to Churchtown to get the car."

I questioned, "How were they going to get there?"

"I don't know," the driver replied. "I think they were going to try to find a state trooper."

At the paved road, an ambulance was waiting to take Caren to the hospital in Pattsville. I went with Caren, and the "MASH unit" took the girls to the Vine Grove emergency station. At the Pattsville Hospital, the nurse said, "Go back to your Girl Scout group. I'll call Caren's Dad and get the necessary permission. Don't worry about insurance papers right now."

Returning to Vine Grove in the ambulance, I found a worried but restless group at the emergency station. The man at the emergency station called the state troopers on the radio to see if Carol and Lisa were there. The trooper said, "They were here, but I couldn't take them to Churchtown until I got off duty."

Now I knew what they meant when the Red Cross first aid class said to get organized before you start action, so everyone is not running in circles. Around five o'clock, Carol, Lisa and Caren drove up in our car. The doctor had told Caren she could travel but not to hike. With the confusion and all the waiting around, everyone's enthusiasm for hiking had waned.

Johanna said, "I don't want to go back and hike. Can I camp by the car until you finish hiking? The Trail in Pennsylvania isn't as exciting as the White Mountains."

Stephannie said, "If Caren can't continue hiking, how will she get home? If she has to go home on a bus, I'll be glad to go with her, so she won't be alone."

"I want to go home too," DeAnna added.

We found a motel and I called Papa. "The group doesn't want to hike any farther," I told him, "Call their parents and tell them we'll be home tomorrow."

While DeAnna waited at my house for her father to pick her up, she said, "I wish we'd stayed on the trail. I feel let down, now that we've come home without finishing."

144

"Try to remember this feeling when you're tempted to quit some future, more major project in your life, DeAnna," I said.

The aborted trip kept bothering me. I had the time, and we had the food and enough gasoline money. Why not go back now and continue? About three A.M. Sunday, I woke Papa and asked him, "If the girls want to go back, is it all right with you if we finish the hike?"

He said, "I think that's a good idea."

At a reasonable hour, I started calling the group. Lisa and Stephannie said they would like to continue, but the others had already made other commitments. Mr. Ness, the owner of a service station in Vine Grove, put us back on the trail on Monday, and we hiked in the rain to the campsite we had picked out the previous Wednesday.

The next day we came to a little store and checked our food supply to make sure we hadn't forgotten anything. Stephannie remarked about her sprained wrist the summer before and said, "If it had been Caren's wrist, she could have continued hiking."

Mark from Maine and a man and his son were at the lean-to. We hung our tent up to dry and spent the evening chatting about Maine. Lisa said, "It's seventeen miles to the next shelter. That's a long hike, but Stephannie and I would like to get there by tomorrow night. We want to finish this section by Saturday."

"Let's see how rough the trail is before we decide for sure. It'll mean some long days in order to finish by Saturday, but I'll sure do my best to help you make your goal," I responded.

We followed old stage roads and creek beds, then climbed to the summit of Stony Mountain and descended into Clark Creek Valley. Coming to a nice creek with a spring nearby, we were ready to camp for the night.

Two days later we crossed Clarks Ferry Bridge over the Susquehanna River, hiked through Duncannon and began the steep climb up Cove Mountain. At Hawk Rock, which protrudes above the trees, we stopped to look down on the town of Duncannon, the Susquehanna River and farmland in the valley. Then we passed Thelma Marks Memorial Shelter, and on to Darlington Shelter, a fifteen mile day.

We had to go a quarter of a mile to the spring where the cool, refreshing water came right out of the mountain. As we ate supper, Stephannie said, "Johanna was telling us about hiking in the White Mountains. She said that group skipped Wildcat Mountain because of bad weather. Did you ever go back and hike that mountain?"

145

"Yes," I answered, "and so far, it's the only part of the Trail I've done without Girl Scouts. I also hiked Mt. Madison then because the first time I had to take an adult around the side of the mountain and didn't get to the summit with the girls."

"How many miles was that?" she asked.

"About five, I think," I answered.

"How much of the trail have you hiked?" asked Lisa.

"All but about a hundred miles," I replied, "Girls have wanted to hike, and it's just sort of happened. Maybe a group will soon want to hike the section I haven't done."

Wanting to finish our trek before the day became too hot, we were on our way at daylight. The Shipe Family, who live along the trail, had spread the word for hikers to stop, share their hiking adventures and have ice cream. Leaving the ice cream lady's home (as she was called along the trail), we hiked on road to Churchtown. As we waited for Mr. Ness, we lay under the shade of a maple tree. "I'm really proud of you," I told the girls, "You've hiked over sixty-eight miles in five days and reached your goal of finishing by Saturday."

"I'm proud of me too," Stephannie said. "I felt disappointed after I got home last week. I'm glad to be a part of your bits and pieces. I think it's great that you're so close to finishing the Trail."

"That's not really my goal," I said, "but sometimes I get so excited, thinking I might just do it, I find it hard to remember my real goal. It's like holding a piece of candy in front of a child." "I think you should go for it, Mama Boots," said Lisa.

CHAPTER FIFTEEN

Erawanda drove us to Bear Mountain Park in New York State. As we were riding along, I recalled how this started sixteen years ago. I thought it would be just one hike in the Smokie Mountains, but the A.T. gave me the opportunity to use my talent to introduce girls who lived in a metropolitan area to the wonders of nature and offered a setting in which they could develop personal values and gain in self-confidence. Some girls developed A.T. fever and wanted to hike as many miles as possible. The eagerness of the girls kept us going.

The news that Mama Boots had only 110 miles to finish on the A.T. spread through the Kentuckiana G.S. Council, and on August 5, we were ready to begin our hike south to the Delaware Water Gap, the final connecting link of the 2000 mile Trail. We had three first time hikers, Kim from Troop 116, Jeanne F., who wanted to try the A.T., and Marie R., a Girl Scout leader who wanted to learn about backpacking. Sherri, Theresa, Lisa P. and Gayla, my adult hiking buddy, wanted to be there when I completed the Trail.

Sherri, Theresa, and Lisa started up Bear Mountain in a hurry. Kim worked hard to keep up, but the steep climb was more than expected. When we stopped for lunch, Kim felt weak and had a stomachache. I asked the group to slow down. We had plenty of time and needed to go slower on the first day.

Shortly after lunch, I caught up with Kim who was sitting on a rock crying. "Do you still have a stomach ache," I asked.

"It doesn't ache anymore," she said, "but it feels very weird."

147

"You've been working hard at being a good hiker, and with the sizable altitude change from Bear Mountain Bridge to the top of Bear Mountain, it could be altitude sickness," I suggested, "Let's rest here and eat some of these delicious looking blueberries."

The next day, Jeanne, Marie, and Gayla hiked together. Lisa, Sherri, and Theresa were way out in front, and I hiked with Kim. As we walked along, I tried to keep Kim's mind off what she was doing, so she wouldn't panic again. The afternoon would be the real test. I wasn't sure where we'd find water, and it could be another long day.

We came to the Lemon Squeezer, a narrow passage between boulders with a steep descend, and Kim seemed to enjoy the challenge of getting down between the boulders with her pack on. When Kim and I caught up with Theresa at four o'clock, she hadn't found water. I told Kim to rest while Theresa, Sherri, Lisa, and I scouted ahead. In about twenty minutes I found water and called "Tongo" to signal the group to come on. We were thankful to have a little time to rest and clean up before supper.

On the third day of the trek, we hadn't been hiking long when Kim became very ill. "I had intestinal flu this summer," she said, "I feel the same way now."

Everyone kept trying to find something to relieve her discomfort, but nothing would stay down, not even plain water. Marie, Gayla, and I decided we'd better try to find a way to get Kim out of the woods before she dehydrated. It started raining, and I suggested to Marie, Gayla, Sherri and Jeanne that they pitch a tent and wait while Theresa, Lisa, and I tried to find Kim a way home. I knew Kim was a very level-headed person, and she assured me her parents would want her to come home under the circumstances. When we got to the main road, I stopped a car. The young lady in the car asked, "Can I help you?"

I told her, "We're a Girl Scout group hiking on the A.T.. Kim is sick and needs to go home."

She said, "I was a Girl Scout. I'll be glad to help."

I asked Kim, "Do you feel comfortable going with the lady?" Kim answered, "I will be all right." The young woman agreed to put Kim on a bus for New York where she could get a plane home.

It had quit raining by the time we got back to the group. I wished we could camp there, but we had no water to prepare food. It was three o'clock, and according to the guidebook, it was 4-1/2 miles, including a couple of mountains to climb, before we reached water. Marie was quite tired, but Jeanne hiked with

Theresa, Sherri, and Lisa. They stopped when they came to water, and the rest of us caught up. A twenty-five foot waterfall between the rocky cliff made a great place to splash, and we managed to clean up and eat supper before dark. When I crawled into my sleeping bag, I prayed Kim had gotten home and would be all right.

The following day, I suggested we hike to Warwick Turnpike, find a motel, get a hot shower, and sleep in a bed. I hoped this would be the solution to our fatigue. At first, the terrain was easy but then we started ascending Oat Rocks, an upturned strata of red-dish conglomerate with the top leveled by glacial action. Then we had to climb another conglomerate outcropping, Eastern Pinnacles. Everyone seemed to be having fun waving to each other between the two peaks, and we came to a spring by lunch time.

About mid-afternoon, we came to a small brook. We had been pushing every day, and Marie and Jeanne needed a short day, but the water was brown and had a bad taste, the result of iron salts leaking through the soil. We continued to the top of an outcropping along the ridge of Bellvalle Mountain and walked along the outcropping with short, steep ascends and descends for over a mile. Marie fell and skinned her leg. She wasn't seriously hurt, but it shook her up. Jeanne was weary and disgusted from walking on the hot rocks, and we all wished we were down swimming in Greenwood Lake. When we reached the end of the outcropping, Lisa, Theresa and Sherri were far ahead.

I decided to try to catch them and figure an alternate plan for the night. I reached a road but still hadn't caught them. When they heard me calling "Tongo" they waited. I explained, "We're going to have to stop. Marie has hurt her knee, and Jeanne is exhausted. I don't think they can make it."

Theresa went back to help Jeanne and Marie so we could make it to the motel, but I was beginning to wonder if this day would ever end. I was extremely tired myself. Lisa and Sherri got to Warwick Turnpike and found someone at a riding stable who would take us to town to the motel. Sighing with relief, we put our packs in the lady's Bronco. Marie said, "Jeanne and I are going to get off the Trail tomorrow. We aren't able to take the long days and hard hiking."

Marie had hiked with me in Jefferson County Forest and Jeanne had backpacked some, but the shortage of water in New York was causing us to hike longer each day than we wanted, and the heat, blasting up from the rocks, also took its toll.

I lit the stove for a hot breakfast, and Marie started making arrangements for her and Jeanne to get home. They were really tired. Jeanne walked up and

I said, "When I was in this same situation in Pennsylvania, I had another girl named Jeannie who felt just like you do. She even said 'I'm going to lay down and die.' We were able to stop and take an afternoon off. I'm sorry we can't do the same for you, but I'm still proud of you for being part of my group of girls who've hiked the A.T. and helped me reach my goal of hiking the Trail with Girl Scouts."

"Thank you, Mama Boots," Jeanne said, "I'm sorry too, but I'm just not prepared for this. Maybe someday I'll pick up the Trail where I stopped."

As the lady drove up to take us back to the trail, Lisa said, "I'd better quit too. My legs hurt really bad."

Theresa started putting our packs in the Bronco and said, "Come on, Mama Boots. Marie can handle the arrangements. We want to continue hiking."

I felt guilty about losing half my group, but before I had time to dwell on mistakes, Theresa, Gayla, and Sherri had me well on the way to finishing the trek. We followed a road most of the day, stopping at houses along the way for water. Much of the Trail in this section was in the process of being relocated onto a protected corridor acquired by the State of New Jersey.

Reaching the end of the road, we climbed the mountain far enough to find a place to put up our tents. We had enough water in our canteens to fix supper. Theresa and Sherri put their socks on the limbs of a shrub to air. It made such an attractive sock tree that Gayla and I put our socks on the shrub also. We sat telling jokes and chatting as we admired our decorated shrub before our last climb of the day, which was into our sleeping bags.

We hiked into Unionville, New York, picked up our package of mailed food, repacked our packs, and gave away the extra food. As we continued our hike, the grass and weeds were wet from rain. Gayla remarked, "The trail here is sure different. It reminds me of the farms in Adair County in Kentucky, plenty of weeds at the edge of the cornfields."

Crossing a stone fence at the edge of the field, I added, "These old rock fences are different too. They were probably built many years ago as field dividers, and this poison ivy around the rocks is sure healthy."

At High Point Shelter, a nearby stream was a perfect place for an Indian Princess bath to wash off the poison ivy. It rained during the night, so when we started hiking, our shoes and socks got wet again. Sherri said, "It's been a week since my feet were dry."

It was just a slow drizzle, and the Trail wasn't strenuous. Arriving at High Point State Park, Theresa called home and found out that her sister, Carmel, was officially engaged. We started reminiscing about how many of the hiking

150

trips either she or one of her three sisters had hiked with me. Margaret was on the first trip and the one over Springer Mountain. Carmel started at Katahdin and hiked to Glencliff, New Hampshire.

Theresa added, "I started there and Carolyn hiked somewhere in North Carolina and Tennessee. I can remember Maggie talking about going backpacking with Mama Boots on the A.T. when I was just three years old."

"Has it been that long?" I asked.

"Yep. Maggie graduated from college, married, had three children, and now teaches elementary school. She's also a Girl Scout leader. She got hooked on Scouting when she went backpacking with you."

"Maggie once told me 'even the hardest, most painful climbs up a mountain, come to an end, and there's no sense worrying. Just put one foot in front of the other, and when the level stretch comes, you'll be back to enjoying yourself,'" Theresa added.

"That's a good philosophy for life," I replied, "I heard from one of the girls who hiked several trips in Virginia, Pennsylvania and Maryland, named Patty, and she told me she'd followed me up mountains for so many miles that when she closed her eyes, she could still see the back of my legs."

"I bet there's a lot of girls who can say that," she laughed, "How many girls have hiked with you on the trail?"

"I counted them up the other day. This trip makes one hundred and thirty-five different girls," I answered.

Our recollections set a nostalgic tone which continued as we hiked. I kept thinking about the different girls and remembered the fun we'd had splashing in mountain streams, singing around campfires and talking about the things that were important to us.

When we reached Anderson Shelter, Theresa read the trail register. It was like the evening newspaper—some hikers had written poetry, others left comical pictures. Some left notes for other hikers they'd met earlier on the trail. Trail conditions and food sources close to the trail were noted for the benefit of fellow hikers who would come along. It told of a bakery three miles away.

Theresa said, "Breakfast in the morning at the bakery shop!"

We made our own entry and signed it "Mama Boots & Company, Kentuckiana Girl Scouts."

After a doughnut feast, Theresa and Sherri started hiking and didn't want to stop. They passed a shelter and creek where we could have camped but kept going until they came to a blacktop road. Gayla and I caught up and found a nearby spring where we camped. It had been a fast thirteen-mile day.

Two more days, and we'd finish the connecting link. Sherri and Theresa hiked ahead, like advance couriers for royalty, telling everyone they met. When Gayla and I would pass these same hikers, they offered congratulations and my excitement really mounted. Six miles from the end of the trek, we stopped to camp. Pitching tents, Sherri and Theresa took my hat made from a red bandanna and went into one of the tents. I could hear them giggling and wondered what was up.

Gayla and I lay in the other tent making plans for another A.T. hike. Gayla had A.T. fever and wanted to hike in the southern section. Hiking with her would give me a chance to hike the bald mountain in North Carolina that had been in the clouds when I was there with the girls, and it would give me a chance to show her Rhododendron Gap, still my favorite part of the Trail.

The next morning the girls gave me my hat. It was decorated with "K.G.S. 2,000 mile A.T. Hiker." The trail around Sunfish Pond, a glacial lake, was rocky at first, but soon we were following a path along a little creek filled with small cascades. This path led us through the Delaware Water Gap recreational area. Crossing a wooden bridge, we came to a road leading to the Delaware River bridge. I thought of Steve, the end-to-ender I'd talked with on top of Katahdin when he'd just finished hiking the Trail. He'd told me it had been his life for several months, and he hated for it to end. I knew now how he felt. That impossible trail I'd discovered in the Shenandoah National Park over twenty years ago had grown to be a part of me.

At the end of the bridge that crossed the Delaware, Theresa and Sherri had put up a bandanna ribbon for me to break through as I finished. Not as dramatic as ending at Katahdin, but it suited my bits and pieces just fine. I found a phone booth to call Papa. "Congratulations!" he said. "We'll have a big celebration when you get home." He also told me that Kim, Marie, Jeanne and Lisa had arrived home okay.

Cleaning up at the Presbyterian Church hostel, Erawanda and Marvin came to get us, and we were on our way to A.T. National Headquarters for my 2,000 mile patch. I bought my patch, which Sherri and Theresa took from me, along with a couple of handkerchiefs I happened to have, and disappeared. They came back and asked Jean Cashin, the receptionist, to come out on the porch with them. There was much whispering and giggling. They sang the *Star Spangled Banner* as Jean tied the hand-made medal around my neck. I'd never really thought of myself as an athlete, but I had run the course through the summits of the mountains. The girls had lovingly fashioned my medal by gluing the patch to the bottom of my Sierra cup and used the hankies as ribbons. They took my

152

dirty hiking shirt and folded it like a flag to conclude our Olympic-styled ceremony. The girls apologized for not having any flowers, but when I arrived home, a vase of flowers was on the table with a card saying "Congratulations from Papa, your number one fan."

*   *   *   *   *

I later wrote to girls who had hiked with me, asking them to share their memories and feelings about hiking on the Appalachian Trail and if they felt their experiences had influenced their lives.

Michelle's letter sums up most of the responses very well.

> I'd never give back a single moment of time on the A.T., even when my feet were freezing or when we ran out of water, because meeting the challenge and experiencing those successes was incredible. The freshness and coolness of hidden mountain springs and the feeling of accomplishment after completing a hike is fantastic, and of course, the camaraderie of hikers creates the opportunity for life long friendships.

I was very surprised when several replies compared hiking the A.T. with childbirth. Carmel wrote:

> I was expecting my first baby. I'd been to the childbirth classes, practiced my breathing techniques, but let's face it—I was scared to death. I admit, I'm a wimp when it comes to thinking about any type of pain. Although I received a lot of advice, the one bit that stuck with me came from my sister, Maggie. She said, 'Sure it's hard. It's hard work and it does hurt. But so does carrying a fifty-pound pack over a mountain. Giving birth isn't any harder than that, and you've already done that.

Theresa described a special experience:

153

On this trip I really started enjoying backpacking for myself. I've hiked on other trips, but this trip has special meanings. I started with a new pair of boots which I thought were broken in, but they were too big and too heavy; I had huge bloody, popped blisters on both heels and had pulled a muscle in my leg (where the leg connects to the hip). The first six steps of everyday were murder on the feet and lifting my leg over rocks and logs was excruciatingly painful, tripping over something because I didn't lift my leg was even worse. Needless to say I couldn't keep up with my buddies, Harriet and Johanna.

One day was particularity bad. We had to go down a very steep, very rough trail just to cross a road and climb rocks straight up the other side. I was hurting so bad I was crying (something I never admitted to). There was no one around that I could see or had seen all morning, and I was getting lonely and just a little scared. By the time I crawled to the top of the mountain, God and I had one heck of a conversation going.

I turned a bend and there were Harriet and Johanna laughing and pigging out in the middle of the biggest blueberry patch you've ever seen! All was right in my world. I hadn't been left behind, my friends were waiting for me, the sun was out and there were all those blueberries!

It no longer mattered that I wasn't the fastest hiker. I slowed down and started to enjoy the trip instead of racing toward a destination. I started to really appreciate the scenery around me. I even looked forward to the quiet times when I could hear myself think and have those long talks with God.

I appreciate the physical challenge of backpacking and always feel a sense of pride and accomplishment when I finish a trip—I did it and I survived!

The Trail continues to call and I now find myself hiking with the children of the girls who started these hikes. Margaret's daughter Amy, her Aunt Theresa, Gayla and her sister Julia, and Tara, a Girl Scout, hiked with me over Wayah Bald in Georgia. It was a beautiful clear day, and I could see the mountains I didn't get to see before. I took Martha's sons, my grandsons Donald and Matthew, on part of the trail following the North Carolina-Tennessee border from Hot Springs, North Carolina to I-40. It was a real thrill to see the excitement of my grandsons as they hiked Match Patch Mountain. Now, Diane has presented Papa and me with a third grandson, Curtis, to someday go hiking with Grandma—in bits and pieces.

APPENDIX A

Hiker	State(s) and Year(s)	Miles
Jeannie Amick	Georgia, North Carolina, Virginia, Pennsylvania, Maine, New Hampshire 1975, 76, 77, 78, 81	671
Suzanne Alton	Virginia, Maine, New Hampshire 1976, 78	228
Karen Baechle	Virginia, Vermont, Massachusetts, Connecticut 1980, 82	195
Beverly Baker	Virginia 1980	55
Donald Baker (Grandson)	Tennessee, North Carolina 1991	34
Gayla Baker (Adult)	Virginia, New Hampshire, Vermont, Connecticut, Maryland, West Virginia New Jersey, New York, Pennsylvania, North Carolina 1981, 82, 83, 84, 85, 86, 87, 88, 89, 90, 91	846
Matthew Baker (Grandson)	Tennessee, North Carolina 1991	34

Hiker	State(s) and Year(s)	Miles
Carol Bauer	Virginia, Georgia, North Carolina 1974, 76	72
DeAnne Bays	Pennsylvania 1982, 83	104
Ann Binford	North Carolina, Tennessee 1972, 73	77
Janet Bischof	Virginia, Georgia, North Carolina, Pennsylvania 1974, 75, 76	225
Lynn Bischof	Virginia 1974	47
Michelle Bouvette	Virginia, West Virginia, Maryland, Pennsylvania, North Carolina 1976, 77	253
Amy Branson	Pennsylvania 1975	75
Drue Branson	Pennsylvania 1975	34
Jody Branson	North Carolina, Tennessee, Virginia 1971, 72	85
Barbara Brennan	Virginia 1976, 79	108

Hiker	State(s) and Year(s)	Miles
Nancy Brickey	Tennessee, Virginia 1969	103
Kim Brodensteiner	New York 1984	25
Michelle Bruer	Virginia 1977	48
Karen Buckheit	New Hampshire 1980	93
Margaret Buckheit	Virginia, Maine, New Hampshire, Vermont 1976, 80, 81	403
Laura Buckner	Virginia 1981	55
Molly Bufkin	North Carolina, Virginia, Tennessee, Georgia 1969, 71, 73	166
Debbie Burkhardt	Virginia 1976, 77	98
Beth Burks	Virginia 1976	50
Donna Burks	Virginia, Maine, New Hampshire 1976, 78	355

Hiker	State(s) and Year(s)	Miles
Harriet Burt	Georgia, North Carolina, Maine, New Hampshire, Vermont, Connecticut, Massachusetts 1976, 78, 81, 82	480
Pam Carrico (hiked with Thumper)	Maryland, Pennsylvania 1977	120
Melody Carter	North Carolina, Tennessee, Virginia 1971, 72, 73	212
Bonnie Clare	North Carolina, Tennessee 1968, 69, 70, 71	208
Caren Clark	Pennsylvania 1981, 82	104
Bonnie Conklin	North Carolina, Tennessee 1970, 71	135
Lisa Davis	North Carolina, Tennessee, Virginia, Georgia 1972, 73, 74, 75	277
Dona Delph	Virginia 1981	55
Shannon Delph	Virginia 1981	55
Debbie Dewey	Virginia 1976, 77	98

Hiker	State(s) and Year(s)	Miles
Gail Dewey	Virginia, Maine, Tennessee, North Carolina 1976, 77, 84, 85, 86	297
Janine Dewey	Virginia 1980	55
Sherion DeWitt	North Carolina, Virginia, Tennessee 1972, 73, 74, 75	205
Ann Dietrick	North Carolina, Virginia 1969, 70, 71	156
Paula Dix	Virginia 1976	76
Evelyn Eades	Virginia 1976	50
Ginny Edwards	North Carolina, Tennessee 1972	46
Jeanne Fenn	New York, New Jersey 1984	42
Margaret Finney	North Carolina, Tennessee 1970	46
Melanie Fitzsimons	North Carolina, Tennessee 1970	46
Carol Frankenburger	Virginia 1979	58

Hiker	State(s) and Year(s)	Miles
Dina French	Virginia 1980	55
Debbie Fugate	Tennessee, Virginia 1969	45
Torri Fuell	Maine, New Hampshire 1978	180
Leslie Fulkerson	Tennessee, Virginia, Georgia, North Carolina 1972, 74	75
Peggy Gonzolaz	North Carolina, Georgia, Maine, New Hampshire, Virginia 1977, 78, 79	276
Diane Gorbandt	Virginia 1977	48
Lisa Gorbandt	Virginia 1977	48
Jennifer Griffis	Virginia 1980	55
Jeane Hanley	North Carolina, Tennessee, Virginia 1971, 72, 73	163
Patricia Hanley	Virginia, North Carolina, Georgia, Maine, New Hampshire 1977, 78	263

Hiker	State(s) and Year(s)	Miles
Dawn Harpole	Virginia 1986	18
Bobbie Hartline	New Hampshire, Vermont, Massachusetts 1981, 82	215
Diane Hartline	New Hampshire 1980	93
Bonnie Hazel	North Carolina, Tennessee, Virginia 1968, 69	86
Melissa Heines	Virginia, West Virginia, Maryland 1983	73
Pam Henry	North Carolina, Georgia 1977	35
Carolyn Herde	North Carolina, Tennessee 1971	49
Carmel Herde	Maine, New Hampshire 1976, 78, 80	398
Margaret Herde	North Carolina, Tennessee, Georgia 1968, 69, 71, 73	144

Hiker	State(s) and Year(s)	Miles
Theresa Herde	New Hampshire, Vermont, Massachusetts, Connecticut, New York, New Jersey, North Carolina 1981, 82, 83, 84, 90, 91	559
Amy Hettinger	North Carolina 1991	39
Joy Higgins	North Carolina, Tennessee 1972	46
Vickie Hopper	Virginia 1977, 79	106
Cindy Hulse	Georgia, Virginia, North Carolina 1974, 76	111
Jenny Juzwick	North Carolina, Tennessee 1970, 71	95
Lynn Karle	Virginia 1974	47
Janet Kurk	North Carolina, Tennessee 1971	40
Mary Ann Kutter	Tennessee, Virginia 1972	45
Emily Lawrence	Virginia 1980	55

Hiker	State(s) and Year(s)	Miles
Sandy Lemons	North Carolina, Tennessee 1986	41
Sheila Lichtefeld	Virginia 1977	48
Ellen Lilly	North Carolina, Tennessee 1970	46
Lisa Lincoln	Virginia 1976	48
Michelle Lincoln	Virginia 1976	48
Kim McConnell	North Carolina, Tennessee, Virginia 1968, 69, 70, 71, 72	275
Ellen McIntee	Tennessee, North Carolina 1968, 71	72
Martha McWilliams	Virginia 1974	47
Donna Mason	North Carolina, Tennessee, Virginia 1971, 72	94
Kathy Meagher	Georgia, North Carolina, Pennsylvania, Maine 1974, 75, 76	358
Sandra Miller	Virginia 1986	18

Hiker	State(s) and Year(s)	Miles
Alice Mitchell	Virginia 1974	47
Carola Mittel	Virginia, New Hampshire, Vermont 1979, 80, 81	289
Theresa Mudd	North Carolina, Tennessee 1972	46
Jacquelynn Murrell	North Carolina, Tennessee 1970	46
Patty Newsome	Virginia, Pennsylvania, Maryland 1974, 75, 76	172
Carol Niehaus	Virginia, West Virginia, Maryland 1982, 83	128
Marie O'Bryon	Virginia 1982	55
Theresa Patterson	Virginia 1986	18
Karen Pickwick	Virginia, Georgia, North Carolina 1974, 75, 76	160
Peggy Pierce	North Carolina, Tennessee 1968, 69, 71	104

Hiker	State(s) and Year(s)	Miles
Sherri Pitts	Virginia, New York, New Jersey, Connecticut, Pennsylvania 1980, 82, 83, 84	352
Lisa Powers	Pennsylvania, New York, New Jersey 1983, 84	135
Wilma Probus	Virginia 1982	55
Tina Rich	Virginia 1976	48
Judy Rogers	Virginia 1985	27
Mary Sue Ryan (Adult)	North Carolina, Tennessee, Virginia 1971, 72, 76	182
Crystal Sanders	Virginia 1976	48
Christy Samuel	Tennessee, Virginia 1972	45
Diane Sands	Georgia, North Carolina, Tennessee, Virginia, Maine, Pennsylvania, Connecticut, New York 1968, 69, 70, 71, 72, 73, 74, 75, 76, 82, 83, 86	1018

Hiker	State(s) and Year(s)	Miles
John Sands	North Carolina, Tennessee, Virginia, Georgia 1968, 72, 73, 74	188
Martha Sands	Virginia, Tennessee, Georgia 1965, 67, 72, 73	83
Suzanne Sauer	Virginia 1974	47
Dora Schneller	Georgia 1976	25
Jean Schnurr	Connecticut, New York 1983	107
Julia Schooler	North Carolina, Tennessee, Virginia 1971, 72	94
Leta Schooler	North Carolina, Tennessee, Maryland, Pennsylvania 1969, 70, 71, 75	177
Tara Shuck	North Carolina 1991	39
Kathy Skaggs	North Carolina, Tennessee 1970	46
Terri Smitch	North Carolina, Tennessee 1973	32

Hiker	State(s) and Year(s)	Miles
Laurie Snowder	North Carolina, Tennessee, Virginia, Georgia 1972, 73, 74, 75	257
Nancy Spatz	West Virginia, Maine, Maryland, Pennsylvania 1977, 78	300
Debbie St.Clair	Tennessee, Virginia, North Carolina 1972, 73	76
Beverly Steman	Pennsylvania 1982	80
Sheryl Sternburg	North Carolina, Tennessee 1970, 71	95
Pam Stickler	North Carolina, Tennessee 1971	40
Patty Summerville	Virginia, North Carolina, Tennessee 1965, 67, 68	66
Jane Thorp (Adult)	Virginia, West Virginia, Maryland, Pennsylvania, Maine, New Hampshire 1976, 77, 78, 79, 80	589
Jessica Thorp	Virginia 1976, 77	156
Jamie Thurmond	North Carolina, Tennessee 1973	32

Hiker	State(s) and Year(s)	Miles
Susan Tomlinson	Virginia, Georgia, North Carolina 1976	73
Mickie Tripp	Georgia, North Carolina 1974, 75	78
Lauri Tucker	North Carolina, Tennessee 1969, 70	107
Ann Ufhiel	North Carolina, Tennessee 1971	49
Joris Unglaub	North Carolina, Tennessee 1968	41
Tammie Vest	Virginia 1981	55
Dawn Vice	Maryland, Pennsylvania 1975	75
Dean Wagner	North Carolina, Tennessee 1972	46
Susan Ware	Tennessee, Virginia, Georgia, North Carolina 1972, 73, 74	107
Lisa Wentzell	North Carolina, Tennessee 1971	49
Mimi White	Georgia 1975	40

Hiker	State(s) and Year(s)	Miles
Stephannie Whitehouse	Pennsylvania 1982, 83	172
Mary Wicker	North Carolina, Tennessee, Virginia, Georgia 1972, 73, 74, 75	210
Colleen Willett	North Carolina, Tennessee 1970	46
Vi Williams	North Carolina, Tennessee 1968, 69	73
Linda Witt	North Carolina, Tennessee 1972	46
Johanna Wolschlog	New Hampshire, Vermont, Massachusetts, Connecticut, Pennsylvania 1980, 82, 83	257
Beverly Zelesky	North Carolina, Tennessee 1969	41

Other Adults

Julia Bailey	Virginia, Pennsylvania, North Carolina, Tennessee 1987, 88, 89, 90, 91	174
Jamie Boone	New Hampshire, North Carolina 1982	36

Hiker	State(s) and Year(s)	Miles
Barbara Davis	North Carolina, Tennessee, Virginia 1973, 74	72
Elaine McElroy Deason	North Carolina, Tennessee 1969	73
Glenna Doss	North Carolina 1991	39
Regina Gonzolaz	Virginia 1979	61
Mayo Lynam	Virginia, West Virginia, Maryland, Pennsylvania 1982, 83, 85, 89	188
Carol Masterson	Pennsylvania 1983	24
Terry McNary	North Carolina 1972	46
Sonnie Reichart	New Hampshire 1980	33
Marie Ruff	New York, New Jersey 1984	43
Paul Sands	North Carolina, Tennessee, Virginia, Georgia 1967, 68, 70, 71, 72, 73, 74	374
Kay Scheidt	North Carolina, Tennessee, Virginia 1971, 72	94

APPENDIX B

Trail Section and Date(s)	State(s)	Miles	Chapter
Riprap Gap to Rockfish Gap 8/4/1965	VA	13.5	1
Cades Cove to Thunderhead Mt. 8/16/1967	NC/TN	14.4	1
Russell Field to Fontana Dam 8/20/1967	NC/TN	12.6	1
Cosby Campground to Davenport Gap 7/13/1968	NC/TN	9.7	1
Newfound Gap to Cosby Campground 8/15/1968 - 8/16/1968	NC/TN	26.2	1
Newfound Gap to Cades Cove 8/18/1968 - 8/21/1968	NC/TN	37.7	2
Hampton to Damascus 6/17/1969 - 6/20/1969	NC/VA	45	3
Nolichucky River to Hampton 6/14/1970 - 6/19/1970	NC/TN	62	3
Davenport Gap to Allens Gap 7/10/1970 - 7/14/1970	NC/TN	46	4
Allens Gap to Nolichucky River 6/11/1971 - 6/15/1971	NC/TN	49	4
Mt. Collins to Fontana Dam 7/8/1971 - 7/12/1971	NC/TN	45	4

Trail Section and Date(s)	State(s)	Miles	Chapter
Hampton to Damascus 6/10/1972	NC/TN	45	3
Davenport Gap to Allens Gap 8/14/1972 - 8/19/1972	NC/TN	46	4
Davenport Gap to Newfound Gap 4/7/1973	NC/TN	31	5
James River to Rockfish Gap 8/7/1973 - 8/14/1973	VA	72	5
Amicalola Falls to Neels Gap 12/26/1973 - 12/30/1973	GA	40	7
Dicks Creek Gap to Wallace Gap 4/13/1974 - 4/17/1974	GA/NC	35	7
Damascus to Teas 6/6/1974 - 6/11/1974	VA	47	6
Neels Gap to Dicks Creek Gap 12/28/1974 - 12/31/1974	GA	38	7
Wallace Gap to Fontana Dam 4/13/1975 - 4/18/1975	NC	55	7
I-70 to Churchtown, PA 8/11/1975 - 8/19/1975	MD/PA	75	8
Amicalola Falls to Neels Gap 12/26/1975 - 12/30/1975	GA	40	7
VA 652 to James River 4/10/1976 - 4/16/1976	VA	50	9

Trail Section and Date(s)	State(s)	Miles	Chapter
Damascus to Teas 6/13/1976 - 6/18/1976	VA	48	6
Roaring Brook to Monson 7/28/1976 - 8/9/1976	MA	125	9
Dicks Creek Gap to Muskrat Shelter 12/27/1976 - 12/30/1976	GA/NC	27	7
Sinking Creek Mt. to VA 652 4/11/1977 - 4/16/1977	VA	50	10
Wallace Gap to Dicks Creek Gap 12/26/1977 - 12/31/1977	NC/GA	35	7
Monson to Gorham 7/22/1978 - 8/13/1978	MA/NH	180	10
Pearisburg to Craig Creek 4/8/1979 - 4/13/1979	VA	58	11
Elk Garden to Big Walker Tower 6/12/1979 - 6/19/1979	VA	61	11
Big Walker Tower to Pearisburg 4/7/1980 - 4/11/1980	VA	55	11
Gorham to Glencliff 7/10/1980 - 7/23/1980	NH	91	12
Rockfish Gap to Lewis Mt. 4/5/1981 - 4/7/1981	VA	53	11
Glencliff to VT 11 7/26/1981 - 8/9/1981	NH/VT	135	13

174

Trail Section and Date(s)	State(s)	Miles	Chapter
Lewis Mt. to Front Royal 4/11/1982 - 4/15/1982	VA	54	11
Delaware Water Gap to Port Clinton 6/11/1982 - 6/18/1982	PA	78	14
Mt. Madison and Wildcat Mt. 7/22/1982 - 7/24/1982	NH	20	15
VT 11 to Salisbury 8/10/1982 - 8/21/1982	VT/CN	140	13
Front Royal to I-70 4/2/1983 - 4/9/1983	VA/WV/MD	73	11
Port Clinton to Churchtown 6/13/1983 - 6/15/1983	PA	92	14
Salisbury to Hudson River 8/8/1983 - 8/16/1983	CN/NY	105.5	13
Hudson River to Delaware Water Gap 8/5/1984 - 8/14/1984	NY/PA	110	15